Sensitivity Girl

LuAnn Billett

LAB Photography Press
Litiz, Pennsylvania

Published by LAB Photography Press.

Library of Congress Cataloging-In-Publication Data
Sensitivity Girl / LuAnn Billett — 1st ed.
ISBN: 978-0692080627
eISBN:
WC: 62,614
1. Memoir. 2. Family Drama. 3. Literary.

Cover design by Joel Holland: http://jmhillustration.com/
Epigraph by Shearwater: http://shearwatermusic.com/
Formatted in beautiful Missoula, Montana
Printed in the U.S.A.

Publisher info:
Website: http://www.labphotographylab.net/

Cyndi,
To my new best
friend + soul mate.
It was amazing
to meet you + we
need to connect
again soon.

♡

Luc

For my children.
Without you, I would still be a struggling mortal.

"Stay away from old thoughts old doubts and old feelings.

But keeping it so far down isn't easy

And you know it's too late

Late for a last war

And it's too late

To back out of your real life."

— Shearwater, *Wildlife in America*

Sensitivity Girl

FOREWARD

When our mutual friend, Jen, called me on the phone in my sixth grade reading class, the students watched my immediate reaction. "...LuAnn needs her friends right now." I walked out of my classroom and rushed to Sensitivity Girl's bedside; it was an emergency. With no memory of the drive to her new house or even the words we said at the time, love's gravity pulled me to my superhero and friend.

As the life altering moments unfolded during those early October days, Sensitivity Girl would exercise strength to confound witnesses, a town would rally to help her, and three babies would grow in a home devoid of sadness.

Our journey together began long before her days of greatest challenge. I am her super sidekick, Impulse Boy. I will never shy from reacting. Unfortunately my knee-jerk tendencies preclude awareness of potential destruction. Thankfully, Sensitivity Girl has a rescuer's heart; she taught me to better assess collateral damage before my undertakings. She showed me truth and kindness must be in balance in our attempts to save the day. If we are kind for only kindness's sake, we mislead by providing false security. At the same time, we can be annihilatingly truthful, as we lay others in ruin. Balance is best.

Sensitivity Girl recounts LuAnn's heroic journey from the earliest recollections to the transitions of many life-stages and challenges. Her insight to the human condition borders on universal, while the narrative pours like a favorite coffee drink. In this story the key players take their places, play their roles, and urge our hero to use her sensitivity super powers. When the dust settles, the powers of good triumph despite repeated blows that would lead lesser characters to surrender.

As a valued player in this epic, I can attest to its accuracy and poignancy. I beam with laser-like pride as I drink in my friend's well crafted composition that she has infused with experience, wisdom, and most important, truth balanced with kindness.

Shane Long

Chapter 1

Some heroes are born with super powers. Others develop their powers over time, or through a specific incident or accident. Many super heroes are outcasts or oddballs, different from the people around them. Most have no choice in their hero destiny. My own powers come from aspects of all of the above. Especially the oddball part.

Some of my favorite early memories are of pretending to be a single father. Dressing my dolls, feeding them, putting them down for naps, just like other girls my age. However, at the time, I didn't even think it was weird—when I was playing with dolls, I distinctly remember pretending to be a single dad. While many girls my age were fantasizing about becoming beautiful, confident, loving mothers like Claire Huxtable or Mrs. Brady, I seemed to take my inspiration from the balding Mr. Drummond from Different Strokes.

Another early memory is a kickball game in our yard with my older brother Kevin and his friends on a sweltering summer day. When they all started stripping off their shirts, I did too. I think I had a full sixty seconds of topless joy before my mother intervened and told me to put my shirt back on. I was confused. Why did I have to wear a shirt while all the other kids, who happened to be boys, could run free? It was the first of many messages telling me boys followed different rules than girls.

I didn't limit my masculine identities to father figures and shirtless footballers. When riding my bike, I liked to wear imitation leather gloves and imagine I was a motorcyclist in a stunt show. I'd ride my bike as fast as my little legs would allow toward a bump at the end of our driveway which would launch the bike and me up into the air. In reality, I may have only gotten about one or two inches of lift, but in my mind, I was soaring several feet above an adoring crowd. Other times I would crawl into my closet with a collection of products I stole from the bathroom cabinet. I'd randomly mix the liquids together and pretend I was a mad scientist, male of course, inventing an evil serum. I never wanted to be a princess; I wanted to be either the guy rescuing her, or the guy who locked her up.

Freudians of the world may be disappointed to learn I never *actually* wanted to be a boy. I never once wished I could grow a beard or write my full name effortlessly in the snow by simply pulling down my trousers. My choice of alter egos was simply my way of imagining myself as a much stronger, much more independent person than I really was. The boys I knew seemed to just be born that way, with freedom and confidence, and I was jealous.

The real me, the day-to-day LuAnn, was afraid of everything. Bridges, loud noises, sewer grates, shadows, movie witches, big dogs, those bugs that look like bushy eyebrows, heights, strangers...even short people terrified me. The tax lady in our town was a tiny woman, like 4'5". One evening when I was around four, my father took me along with him on a visit to her office. I screamed so much because of this scary little woman that my dad made me wait on the porch until he was finished. Another time, I stayed over at my grandparents' house and sobbed the entire night because I was 100% convinced I was being kidnapped by my own sweet, gentle grandparents. I thought they were going to keep me forever.

With reality out of my control and always looming around me, I felt like the only place I had any power was in my fantasy life. But why did it seem like I'd been afraid from the womb? I lived in a small suburban town in Pennsylvania, in a safe home in a safe neighborhood. Most of our neighbors not only kept their cars unlocked, some left the keys in them. It wasn't like my day to day existence was especially frightening.

Turns out it wasn't fear I was born with; it was an inoperable case of relational and emotional sensitivity.

Experiences, feelings, and reactions are intensified for me. It is a little like living life in super high definition.

For as long as I can remember I have been able to read the emotions of other people. With about 90% accuracy I can tell, sometimes from across a room, if someone is overwhelmed, happy, uncomfortable, angry, excited, hungry, nauseous, nervous, insecure, etc.... What it also means is I'm acutely aware of how the person I am talking to is feeling about *me*. I know if you're happy with me, attracted to me, pissed at me, or generally dislike me. But I don't just read emotions, I FEEL them. Strongly, deeply, even when they aren't mine.

For a very long time I was not happy about having powerful sensitivity. There was one Christmas morning when everyone else got an Atari gaming system and I got a disappointing sweater. It felt like everyone else my age was blissfully playing Ms. Pac Man while I was sitting around in my stupid wool pullover trying to fake gratitude so as not to hurt anyone's feelings. Back then I couldn't appreciate the merits of its warmth or artfully knitted weave. I would have much rather had the video game system.

Yes, being Sensitivity Girl could suck, and it usually did. It was way worse than The Cypher or that Wonder Twin who could only change into various forms of water

—which, if you're familiar with water, there are pretty much two: frozen and liquid. There is steam I guess, but I don't recall him using that one. Sensitivity, on the other hand, means you know how people are feeling and you can usually figure out why. It hits hardest, and it often feels like you *are* the reason. And because you sense this stuff, but can't change it, the best way to deal with it, especially as a child, is to try going invisible. I would have given anything to exchange my power of sensitivity for invisibility. But when it comes to natural born gifts there is no return period, no exchanges, no refunds.

The best time in my young life was during what would normally be the pre-school years. Instead of sending me to pre-school every day my mother took me to the library, Mommy-and-Me swim classes, and shopping. Once a week we would have lunch in the restaurant of a local, fancy, department store. During those outings, those one-on-one times with her, I felt so special. I also felt like I had the best mom in the entire world. I never wished I had gone to pre-school instead. So why, when I was alone in my room with my dolls, did I imagine I was a single dad?

While normal, even idyllic on the outside, the truth of my upbringing was one of severely mixed messages. I was the only natural child in my family. I came along in the winter of 1973, a few years after my older brother and sister had been adopted. From early in their marriage my parents had been told my mother would never be able to conceive. My father was unbending in his wish to raise children, so adoption had been their best option at the time. When my mother did finally become pregnant, even though the odds were not in our favor, she was able to carry me to term.

Adoption is hard enough on parents and children without adding a natural child to the mix and creating an even more complicated dynamic. My mother was overjoyed to have me in her life, but her happiness also caused her guilt and concern. My sister and brother deserved to receive the same depth of emotion from her, but it didn't occur as naturally. While I felt my mother's love to a degree, I could perceive her anxiety as well. She had a goal of creating a level playing field, and it was always very important to her that things between the kids be equal and fair.

My mother had been the oldest of four children. Her mother suffered from mental illness which worsened as time passed. Mother remembers her early childhood as happy, but when her siblings were born, my grandmother's erratic behavior and irrational emotions became more of a burden on her and her younger brother and sisters. I think my mother just wanted things to be smoother and more consistent for her own children. Yet emotions and feelings are very difficult to control and regulate, especially regarding family.

I understand it better now, but as a child I could not ignore my siblings' feelings of insecurity toward my existence. Occasionally, my brother would tell me how I was "free," an accident, but that my parents paid lots of money for him. I never retaliated or cried and ran to my mommy. Even as a little kid I knew his words were coming from his own uncertain feelings. I could feel his torment. I also knew that bringing this to my mother would force her to confront her own conflicted feelings and anxieties.

My brother and sister might be surprised to learn I interpreted things this way. I am sensitive, not psychic. Their experience of reality was probably a lot different than mine. I only knew what I sensed from them. It was a daily thing, this feeling that I caused others pain. As a child it was incredibly hard to bear.

I don't have many memories of fighting with my siblings, because fighting with people I love is even more painful than tuning in to their normal everyday feelings. Insight also comes with the ability to devise deep, personally biting things to say to someone. Sensitive people can easily tap into the inner life of others, and this means understanding their weaknesses and insecurities. Because of added understanding I can be a kind, caring friend, but I also have the potential to be the worst nightmare during times of conflict. I mainly chose to push down those awful thoughts and absorb the anger rather than intensify the conflict. Anger, including my own, is something I always wanted to hide or avoid.

What felt like a minor benefit at the time was my ability to discover sensitivity in others. Most would become friends who would be in my life for decades. These sensitive companions have provided both strength and comfort. There are a few, additionally, who had something even more distinctive: a spirit and presence that hit me deeper than friendship. When I was young, around age ten, I met one of these distinctive people. A boy so special, so sensitive, so super, he would impact the entire course of my life.

Chapter 2

I learned early on that I could not rely only on friendship to give me strength. I had to develop some other strategies to survive. I tried to build up my strength in sports. My older sister was a natural athlete. She was one of the only girls in our town who could hit a home run over the fence at our local softball field. It seemed everyone in town knew about her talent. My father loved going to her ball games, and even more so, loved bragging about her accomplishments to his work friends. She seemed so happy and confident. I hoped that maybe sports could be the key to winning over my father and feeling good about myself.

My earliest memories of my father relate to my failures, and more specifically, his disappointment in my failures. These failures could be anything from spilling a glass of water to shutting a door too hard. He had this way of talking to me and looking at me like I was the clumsiest, most clueless person on the planet. It was hard for me to live with the quiet feelings of my siblings, and it was unbearable to live with my father's very clear messages of dissatisfaction in me.

It turned out I was not the natural athlete my sister

was. Not even close. My father expected me to play softball because he had played baseball as a kid. He liked the sport and understood it. I don't even remember it being a choice for me. Unfortunately, I was terrible. I spent two miserable summers standing in right field, alone, squinting into the burning sun and wishing I were anywhere else. I was uncoordinated, and worse, terrified of flying projectiles. I prayed the balls would land as far from me as possible. I didn't even have to use my super power to read my father's disappointment; he would share this information willingly. My father tried urgently to help me become a better player, but his unique teaching approach included too many phrases such as, "How will you ever improve if you insist on throwing and running like a girl?"

Later, to please him, and because I was tall, I tried basketball. He'd been on a State Championship basketball team in High School, so he was even more jazzed about this than softball. However, sensitive people like me do not do well in sports where other people are doing unpredictable things and trying to keep *you* from doing things. I could dribble, and even shoot baskets well—at least until a stranger came barreling towards me at full speed. If this was going to work I needed to find a zero-contact physical outlet where I had maximum control over most of the parameters.

After a few years of utter misery, I couldn't take it anymore. I could no longer spend my free time playing sports I hated. Behind his back, with the help of one of my friends' moms, I signed up for the local summer swim team. It was very unlike me, to do anything against my parents' wishes. I was just so desperate to do something I enjoyed. My feelings about ball sports were bad enough to risk either punishment or additional paternal disappointment.

Many parents either think or pretend to think every blessed thing their child does is spectacular and genius. Every poop, every scribble, every mud pie is a freaking masterpiece. My father was never one of those parents. He appreciated measurable success, and not only were my mud pies far from award winning, my swimming skills were barely chart-able.

"You can't possibly enjoy your swim meets," he'd say. "Doesn't it embarrass you, coming in last all of the time?" Translation: "I don't enjoy your swim meets. I am embarrassed that you come in last all of the time."

No lie, early in my career I was probably the worst swimmer in our town—maybe in the whole state. I was one of those kids who flailed across the pool, banged into the lane lines a few times, and eventually came up sputtering on the other end. My swimming competitors were often completely dry, changed, and eating snacks by the time I pulled myself out of the water. I am convinced I earned last place in every race I swam during my first year on the team.

Astonishingly, my shameful swimming skills and my father's steady stream of disparaging remarks did not discourage me from riding my 10-speed bike across our town to the pool every summer morning. I loved the swim team and everything that went along with it. I enjoyed the practices almost as much as the meets. The time in the pool, even when it was filled with other swimmers, allowed me to experience a quiet and meditative state I have yet to find elsewhere. When I was swimming, I felt like I belonged in the water. The pool provided a sensory deprivation situation where I could mute my sensitivity and find peace from the constant barrage of emotions that came from my interactions with people on land.

I also had my eye on one of the team swimmers. It wasn't just because he was, without a doubt, the cutest boy I had ever met. It wasn't just because no one really knew him, and he kept to himself in a very James Dean-esque sort of way. He was the type of swimmer I could only dream of becoming. When Chris swam, it looked like he was moving in slow motion—effortless. He could beat every competitor by a full body length or more. I counted the moments to every swim meet just so I could watch him glide through the water, and hope maybe, just maybe, he would talk to me.

Looking back, it's clear there was even more to my crush than his looks or his swimming. Chris had an alluring combination of strength and vulnerability. I had plenty of crushes both prior to meeting Chris and after. Yet there was something different about him and something unique about how I felt around him. He was a powerful swimmer, but he also seemed a bit sensitive. Was he also a reluctant super hero? I wanted to get close enough to him to find out. I didn't realize my chances were slowly slipping away.

He had started on our team as a young kid, but his family eventually moved about 45 minutes away to a completely different county. He felt connected to the team, so while he swam for the bigger, more competitive team in his town, he continued to swim with us at most of our meets. I don't remember him ever earning less than a first place in any race. To my naïve mind, it seemed like such a positive situation, having him help us out at the meets.

Many of the girls my age had crushes on him. He

was the cute boy from a different town who swam like a rock star. Of course, the boys probably weren't as excited about having him there. More specifically, the mothers of the boys he beat at every meet were not at all happy about having him on our team. It was pretty much a given that if he was in a race, the best anyone else could do was second place.

Three years after I joined the team, the helicopter moms finally pushed hard enough to have rules created to keep kids from out of town off our team. Chris was forced to quit our club. Yet the few short moments during the few short years I had with him on the swim team stuck with me for a very long time. There was a connection between us that I did not fully understand but could not forget. I would see him again someday. Yet, I would have to get through a little heaven and quite a bit of hell before that day would come.

Chapter 3

I collected quite a few reluctant super heroes into my circle in the years after Chris left my swim team. I tend to be drawn to people who possess a combination of strength, talent, a unique form of sensitivity, and a dram or more of damage. Mostly friends, and a few more than friends. I can't always explain how or why, often early on, I get a feeling about a person, a vibe, and I must attempt to pull them into my little world of, super sensitive friends. My *Homo sapiens superior.* Once they are in my club, there is very little they can do to escape. It is a lifetime membership.

One of my main sidekicks is my friend Shane. Shane began teaching middle school at the boarding school where I teach photography. When I first saw him, I thought he looked like a guy who taught Sunday school and maybe played an acoustic guitar with a strap covered in peace frog buttons. In his sweater vests and brown loafers, he just looked very very normal. "Normal" people didn't usually "get" me or want to, so while I was nice to him, I didn't go out of my way to get to know him.

It took a few months but eventually I learned how wrong I had been. Shane was not only super weird, he was super funny. Like, inappropriately funny. He was also very open and sincere. If there is a common thread among my closest confidants it is sincerity, and Shane's got buckets of it.

Like me, he is also a bit damaged. His damage just comes in a more visual form. Shane was born with bilateral microtia. In simple terms, Shane was born without ears. While it must have been incredibly hard for him as a child, it is the only life he has ever known. Doctors were eventually able to construct ears from tissue harvested from other parts of his body, but they look a bit different than average ears. He has also had to wear different types of large hearing aids throughout his life.

Shane has never been able to hide the thing that makes him different. The benefit is he had been able to come to terms with it faster and more completely than people with more hidden struggles. Shane had learned to accept what made him unique and found a way to be comfortable in his own skin. He wasn't afraid to be himself, and he also wasn't afraid to stand up for himself. I not only wanted him to be my friend, I wanted to learn how to be more like him.

I was in my mid- 20's when I met Shane, and while I had grown quite a bit from the girl who wanted to be invisible, and had toughened up as well, I still had a long way to go to become a true super hero. I still shied away from conflict, and simply did my best to avoid difficult people. I also naively believed that in a school, a professional setting, all I would have to do is be nice and work hard, and things would be smooth sailing.

I had fallen in love with photography in college. I connected to the shooting, the processing, and the printing instantly. It can be a very introspective, and somewhat solitary art form. The darkroom, like the pool, is a sensory deprivation place. I shot and printed obsessively, which lead to strong and interesting photos. I gained a reputation as one of the best photography students in my peer group. I'd finally found a skill I could truly be proud of.

I had been working at the girls boarding school for a few years teaching photography prior to Shane being hired. I had confidence in my teaching and knew my subject well for a young teacher. However, I quickly found that there were a few difficult personalities among the faculty. No matter how nice I was, and how hard I worked, these people tended to kick me around. Throwing minor mistakes in my face, or just generally being unkind to me.

About a year into our friendship Shane witnessed a common interaction with one of the difficult teachers.

The older teacher and I were planning a field trip together. I had originally thought the museum opened at a certain time, but recently learned it opened earlier, which could make the day's schedule smoother. I was sharing this with my colleague and she immediately tore into me.

"You said it opened at 10am, but now you are saying it is 9:30am?"

"Um, I said I thought it opened at ten, but when I called for tickets the woman told me we could come at 9:30am."

"It's called COMMUNICATION, LuAnn!" she yelled.

"I'm sorry," I said quietly. "I could change it to ten, but I was thinking if we arrive at 9:30am we won't have to cover classes for the extra half hour."

"Leave it at 9:30, but next time get your information straight before we start planning."

She said this loudly and stormed away. She was barely out the door before Shane started laying in to me.

"What the hell was that? She treated you horribly and you just flipped over and showed her your belly?! You apologized and had nothing to apologize for. I never want to see you take that from anyone ever again."

I began to cry. He was right. I was an adult, and I

shouldn't have put up with bullying. Especially from a colleague. Yet growing up, standing up for myself only seemed to make things worse. I had survived for so long by avoiding conflict, I didn't really know how to handle it. For over 20 years, I could operate in a fairly conflict free mode most of the time. I was really good at either avoiding conflict or preventing it. As an athlete I just had to do whatever the coach told me, work hard, and swim fast. As a student I simply showed up for class, on time and prepared, and met every deadline. Even in my first job in a restaurant, which I held from High School through college, I just worked hard and did what I was told. I was easy to deal with and do my job.

I was a bit shocked as my long-term method of operation did not seem to work as well in the professional, educational realm. It was more like typical high school than my own high school experience had been. In high school I was a bit of the weird art room girl, but at the same time I got along with most people. I didn't get bullied. For the most part, people left me alone. At the school where I was employed however, there was an established clique of teachers, and I was not part of that clique. They seemed to always be in a position to pounce on any perceived screw up or flaw. Even when they weren't overtly nasty to me, my sensitivity revealed the plain and simple fact that these people did not like me.

As a child, for as long as I can remember, I wasn't treated with respect by my father. I also learned early on that standing up to him only escalated things. Arguing with him just made him angrier. This was because he had power over me. I was a kid. I needed him. I also felt that maybe I deserved to be treated that way because I wasn't good enough.

So, when those experienced, older teachers treated me poorly, I think I figured I deserved it. I was a good teacher, but maybe not as good as they were. They had been at the school longer and seemed so sure of themselves, at least on the surface. I believed that they somehow had power over me, so I just took whatever they dished out.

I loved my job, however, despite the nasty adult bullies. I was being paid to teach photography to groups of bright, motivated teenage girls. I was in charge of a full darkroom and had access to supplies and equipment that I could never afford on my own. I would meet professional photographers and they would tell me how lucky I was. When I wasn't teaching, I could make photographs that I was interested in making, and I never had to please clients. In addition, the students and the administration seemed to like me very much, and those were the only opinions I should have cared about.

Everything began to change the day Shane called me out for my wimpy behavior. I had built up strength from years of being a good photography teacher. I knew in my heart that I deserved to be at that school, and I did not deserve to be treated like I had been. Yet my default setting was still that of a little girl who was never quite good enough. Shane showed me I had to change my default.

So, cautiously at first, I began to stand up for myself. I didn't yell, I didn't treat people poorly. I just stopped taking their shit. I learned to call people out when they tried to intimidate or belittle me. I learned to stand up for ideas I had that deserved to be considered. I walked a little taller, and I no longer shied away from conflict.

And you know what? It worked. Not magically, not overnight. But it worked. Early on, every single time I would stand up for myself I would call either Shane or my mom and tell them all about it. I needed their emotional support. It was also a bit scary the first few times, facing the bullies. Eventually, as it kept working, as the world did not end when I stood tall, it was no longer scary. It felt amazing.

That day in the faculty room, Shane gave me the push I needed. Standing up to those people was a huge step for me. It not only felt good, but those same individuals started treating me with more respect. Through my sensitivity powers, I could still tell they didn't like me all that much. Yet, it didn't matter. I didn't necessarily like them either. It was only important that they treated me like the professional colleague I was. It didn't turn off my sensitivity, it didn't end bad treatment or conflict in my life. Learning to stand up for myself gave me the skills to fight the even tougher battles on the horizon.

Chapter 4

Fall, 2002. I was 29, alone in my apartment, and the phone was ringing. Because I knew who was on the other line, the sound of the phone suddenly reduced me to feeling like that silly, uncoordinated little girl from high school. Through a church connection between his grandmother and my mother, Chris, epic super hottie from swim team, had my phone number and was calling me. I can't recall the exact transcript of the conversation, but what I do know is that I resorted to my unfortunate nervous habit of uncontrolled babbling and swearing. Somehow, between obscenities, he agreed to meet me for coffee. I'm not sure if it was out of curiosity or perhaps from an intense fear this woman with the mouth of a longshoreman would kick his adorable ass if he didn't.

I didn't know what to do with myself. I paced around my kitchen in a combination of exhilaration and pure panic. I called my best friend and swapped my normal voice for the voice of an awkward middle schooler who just got asked to the winter formal by a 14-year-old version of David Beckham, sans tattoos.

"Oh my gosh, Shane, he was the finest, cutest boy I ever met. He also had the most adorable butt! I can't believe that he called me. ME! I have a date with *the hottest guy on the swim team!*" Then the vain part of me asked: "What if he is fat now? Or a huge nerd?" Shane calmed me down and reminded me that I didn't have to marry this guy; it was just a date.

A few days later, there was a knock at my door. There he was, the adult version of Chris in the flesh. He was still adorable. He still had it. It's so hard to put in to words what made this guy superior to other humans in my mind. While I understand emotional insight, the experience is not easy to define for others. Adjectives rarely do the job. It's a gut thing, a vibe. Many times, it is simply the level at which I am drawn to a person or repelled. It is a little like describing why you like certain music. Sometimes it just comes down to how you feel when the song plays. What I do know is that when I was around Chris, even at a young age, a spectacular song was playing. When I like a song, I want to listen to it on a continuous loop, forever.

The older Chris wore glasses, and though he was only a few months behind me in age, he looked more innocent somehow. For the first hour or so he seemed to look only at his shoes and never directly at me. I worried that perhaps he'd changed his mind. *Maybe I do swear too much?* As he continued to study his feet I became convinced he was plotting an escape.

But this nervous rabbit quality about him made him so much more endearing than I even remembered. As we walked down the street, I kept expecting him to scamper away and hide in the bushes. I tend to be loud, borderline obnoxious when I am nervous. I flail my arms and hands when I talk. I tried to tone down my speech and arm movements, so I wouldn't startle him or send him away screaming in terror. I've often been described as both intimidating and just plain "too much" by shy or reserved people, so I tried my best to keep my fear inducing tendencies and abhorrent qualities in check.

I must have done something right because our date lasted for hours. He captivated me because he shared so much about himself, but at the same time he continued to have trouble looking at me. He was sort of an enigma. He talked about swimming, told me about a painful breakup after a long relationship, his family, both good and bad. I shared a lot, too. The ups, the downs, and craziness of the previous fifteen years of my life came pouring out. I found myself wanting to keep talking to him forever. To hear what he was thinking and feeling about virtually any subject. I felt like I could tell him almost anything. I was getting the exact same vibe from him that I had as a kid on the swim team. That beautiful song was still playing in my head and my heart.

However, I was holding something back. After the evening ended I kicked myself for not asking the big question, but I was too scared. *Did he really remember me? I mean, really remember?*

Before we knew it, it was almost midnight. I was just so comfortable with him that I didn't want it to end. It almost felt strange for him to leave. Instead, I walked him to his car and he shook my hand. It was a bit incongruous. I suddenly felt as if we were concluding a very successful job interview. For maybe the first time ever, my epic sensitivity could not decode the feelings of another person, which was simultaneously exhilarating and frustrating.

The strong basis for my internal conflict stemmed from the fact that the last time I had seen him had been an extremely significant time in my life. Perhaps, one of the most significant of my entire existence. I was certain he didn't remember, and certainly it couldn't mean much to him if he did remember. It wasn't just because the last time I had seen him I was still in that gawky middle school stage and was not the most attractive girl in town. It was because what happened that night was burned into my memory.

Back when I joined the swim team my life at home

was unbearable most of the time. It is challenging to describe all of the details as an adult because honestly, I didn't really understand what was going on with my family at that point in my life. What I do know is there was a lot of conflict, which mostly involved my brother and my father. The conflicts were angry, loud, and sometimes violent. I never knew what each day would bring. I loved my brother very much and had always looked up to him. To see him so angry and out of control was both sad and scary for me. Especially when the rage was directed my way. No matter what I did it always seemed to be a mistake. It felt like every problem in my home was my fault. I was too young to understand how little power I truly had over any of it, in any way.

However, the power of intuition combined with observation made me aware that my home life was not "normal." I felt like we were living in a war zone without the benefit of air raid sirens to warn of the next bomb drop. I knew regular families were not supposed to function this way. I didn't feel comfortable having friends over to my house very often. When I did have a friend over, there would always seemed to be some sort of angry or downright embarrassing scene. Though my friends seemed okay, I couldn't handle it. When I was at a someone else's home I noticed that no one seemed jumpy, and the mothers didn't have sadness or fear in their eyes. Other houses in my town in the 1980's just seemed so calm and happy.

It was difficult for me to watch my mother suffer through constant chaos and drama. I was so connected to her that even at a young age I was tuned in to her desire for a peaceful home life. It clearly hurt her very much that her family and household were so out of her control. I constantly prayed to God for things to get better. For the longest time, or what seemed like the longest time, things only got worse and worse. I would ask my mother questions like, "Why can't we have a normal family?" and "What have we done to deserve this?" or "Why does God hate us?" She didn't have any helpful answers. At the time, I didn't have the life experience to understand things eventually can and do get better. For me it seemed like life would always be that way, which felt unbearable. Now, as a mom, I can only imagine my own mother's torment and suffering.

Eventually I became a better swimmer, and while lap swimming still provided a needed escape; I was also able to collect some self-esteem from winning races. When you feel ashamed and apologetic for things that are truly out of your control, an undeniable win in a competition is very important. A blue ribbon that proves you were the best in a race, that you did a great job, is so incredibly rewarding. The more I won the more I loved my time with the swim team, and the more I could avoid the battleground at home. I started feeling like I might be okay and felt like I had some value too. I vividly remember virtually every race I ever won, and certainly the earliest ones. In many ways, swimming saved my soul and self-esteem.

But the most noteworthy moment, proving I was worth more than I felt, didn't come in a race or a swim meet. I was in seventh grade and our team had just wrapped up the best season we'd had since I joined. I was on top of the world after winning two major races at the championship event and taking home two beautiful trophies. At the end of each season, our parents organized a huge picnic complete with food, awards, games, and a sleepover for all the swimmers. It was always the highlight of our summer, but this picnic was even better because we had done so incredibly well all season. We had a lot to celebrate that night.

I'm not sure why or how it all happened. Maybe it was something in the air, perhaps it was the energy and the high I was feeling from all those wins. Something gave me the courage to finally talk to Chris. I wish I could remember what we talked about. I was so mesmerized by him I probably didn't make much sense regardless of the topic. Later in the evening as the sun set, we all played games, which mostly consisted of silly races across the pool. Somehow, I found myself beside Chris in each race. He was funny and playful and liked to cheat to make me laugh. He would pull my leg and wrestle me to hold me back from winning. It was the first and last time in my entire swimming career that I didn't care whether or not I won. My friends and I were all having fun talking and laughing with Chris. It was the first time he really opened to us and we were all happy when he asked his parents if he could spend the night at the pool.

It was a strict rule that boys and girls had to sleep in separate tents, but in the few hours before lights out we could visit any tent we wanted. We all ended up congregating in Chris's tent and someone had the bright idea of playing spin the bottle. We were in Junior High after all and that is what Junior High school kids did. At least in the 80's it was. The kids on my swim team spent so much time together in the summer that we were practically like brothers and sisters. The kisses exchanged were usually very quick pecks through giggles and funny "gross out" sounds. Then, it was Chris's turn to spin, and everything changed.

I couldn't believe it. The look on my face must have

been priceless when the aerosol nozzle of the hairspray bottle we were using stopped right in front of my crossed legs. I couldn't breathe as Chris leaned in to the center of the circle. As my heart beat insanely inside my chest I knew I had to lean in as well. Chris put his lips on mine and gave me the first real, beautiful, electric kiss of my life. I will remember it clearly until the day I die. Everyone in the tent looked stunned, and he leaned back with a huge grin. The next time it was his turn, he simply turned the bottle with purpose and pointed it right at me and kissed me again. It was like a freaking 80's movie where the dorky chick gets the guy. There were so many girls on the team who were cooler and prettier than me, and I think they were just as surprised. Little did I know this would be the last time I would see him for the next 15 years.

Chapter 5

"Are you cheating on me?" I asked my husband in a stern and knowing voice.

"No!" he answered with shock and anger. "Why would you ask that?"

"I found your cell phone bill, and you call this phone number more than two times a day, every day. The calls are always during your lunch break and on your way home from work. I called the number, and it belongs to a woman."

"What!?!" he exclaimed. "You called it! She is a business contact! That is why I talk to her."

I argued the fact that he was never at work when he called her, and he gave me a pile of excuses. I was not convinced at all, but I really couldn't prove a thing. I just had that intuition that women are supposed to be blessed with. That would hardly hold up in a court of law. Besides, what if I was wrong?

Suspecting infidelity and knowing it are two different things.

In my 20's I still did not have a good grasp of the depth of my sensitivity. I tended to doubt the reality of my concerns and suspicions. This carried over from my early life and may have rendered me overly critical and left me unable to trust others. On one hand, I was pretty certain he wasn't being faithful, but I had no proof. I also felt guilty because if I was wrong and he wasn't cheating, it meant I was an insecure, horrible, suspicious wife. Women are told constantly to trust their instincts but that is much easier said than done. Does any woman ever want to believe that the person who swore to spend the rest of his life with only her would pull his pants down and get naked with another woman?

A few weeks later, completely by accident, I discovered more hard evidence of his infidelity on the internet. It was one of those silly married people arguments. He was supposed to pick up dog food while I spent the day volunteering for an arts group. When I arrived home, I found out he'd played around on the computer the entire day and didn't do the one and only thing I had asked. We rarely argued, but I was exhausted and pissed. After a quick verbal scrap, he stormed out the door to buy the dog food. In the heat of the moment, he forgot to log off the computer.

Within one click I found his profile on an adult website that connects men, women, and couples to other people who are looking for sex. It wasn't just a profile; I could tell he'd been contacting and interacting with other users. There were exchanges saved in a folder. It appeared he may have met with at least some of them, and most likely followed through with showing them the "skills" he had outlined in his personal description. I felt sick in the pit of my stomach. I finally had proof of his infidelity, or at the very least his plans for infidelity, but I didn't exactly feel good about it.

My first husband's dual life crumbled after that night. When he arrived home I immediately showed him the computer printout and kicked him out of our apartment. I also found out he had been emailing his "business contact" through a secret email account. The next day I began the humiliating process of telling my family and showed them the profile as well. I felt like I had no choice. I didn't trust anyone to support me without concrete evidence. The nature of his profile shocked them, as they'd had no idea about this side of him. They'd always liked the guy, and I needed them to see I had a valid reason for booting him. This wasn't just a slip up, or some drunken mistake. There was an active pattern of behavior I was dealing with.

It wasn't long before I heard from him again. He wanted to work things out. He kept promising to change. I explained if there was going to be any chance of us staying together he would need to be completely honest about everything, even the smallest detail. Sadly, I caught him in lies almost immediately. I think this was even harder than learning of infidelity—the absolute knowledge that there was little or no hope of ever knowing if he would be honest about anything.

I had always told myself if the person I married cheated on me that I would divorce them on the spot without thinking twice. The reality was quite different. Our families were in so much pain, and so was I. He had wonderful parents, and they were very upset and hurt by it all. Mine were worried how I would make it on my own. My hair was falling out. I was short tempered, lonely, and grouchy. There were many times I considered taking him back just to stop the pain. I finally understood why women sometimes put up with bad relationships.

In the short term it might have been easier just to forgive and forget, but I knew in my heart I could not stay in a relationship without trust, and I saw no evidence that his dishonesty was going to go away. At one point I told him, "I would have to suffer the rest of my life wondering if you were going to cheat again, and you would get to live your life knowing that I never would." It was a very difficult year, and at the age of 27 I was divorced and living on my own.

When I got married I thought I had finally had

relationships and love figured out. When I married my first husband, I thought I had worked out all of my issues and knew exactly what I wanted. He had not been my first long term relationship. At 23 I felt I was smart enough to get married. I had learned from past relationships, but clearly not enough.

In my late teens and early 20's there was Mike. We met while I was home on a Winter break from college and love was the furthest thing from my mind. My friend Chrisa was friends with the lead singer of an Industrial music band. She invited me to see them play in a divey little club. Mike was the keyboard player and I noticed him immediately. He was tall, slim, with light hair, and strong German features.

Mike wasn't just handsome, he was also a very talented musician. He was incredibly passionate about making music and it was thrilling to watch him create industrial songs. He would spend hours composing music and lyrics, and I loved every minute of watching him compose. I have always been drawn to creative people, and I become especially attached to those who can do something that I can't. He was also sensitive. He felt things very deeply, and cared so much about his friends, his family, and his music. His super power was making music that moved people. I fell fast, and I fell hard.

For some reason Mike always seemed to keep me at arm's length. I just wanted to spend as much time as possible absorbing him and it probably made him uncomfortable. Like a permanent groupie he couldn't get rid of. I was a less ballsy version of Sally from Peanuts, and he was my Linus. Mike was a few years older than me, and much more comfortable with himself. I was needy, young, and still trying like hell to figure myself out. He wanted a relationship as an enhancement to his already full life. I wanted a relationship to complete my life and to complete me. It is easy to imagine how it all worked out in the end.

It took me many years to figure out that incredibly sensitive people have trouble with love. It isn't because they can't find it, it is because deep love has the tendency to provide incredible highs, and devastating lows. It is heroin for the sensitive.

Let me explain a bit better. When I am deeply, head over heels in love, any distance from the person, either physical or emotional, is incredibly painful. When I'm with them and they are engaged with me it is fantastic. This constant ping pong between high and low is quite taxing, not only for me, but for the other person as well. Additionally, if there is a situation where the other person is not as deeply in love, the pain is always there in one form or another. It is hard for highly sensitive people like me to understand when the average person does not respond to love as deeply as the sensitive person does.

I've known for most of my life that to feel this range and intensity of emotions is not normal. So, instead of expressing these feelings, even to a friend, my tendency in the past was to pretend everything was fine. It's important to stress that sensitive people are usually not dramatic, and we don't like to call attention to ourselves. It's a personal failure to make any situation worse than it already is. I would always try my best not to rock the boat. Forget my birthday? "Oh, you're busy." Change plans at the last minute? "Let's just re-schedule." I became a doormat made of braided strips of unexpressed emotions. Such a thing is not easy to sustain, even for the strongest of people.

The saddest part about my relationship with Mike is that after three years it was me who decided to break things off. It hurt too much to be in a relationship where things felt so imbalanced. I knew in my heart he just wasn't as nuts about me as I was about him. I couldn't change him or me, and I knew we would both be better apart. I knew I was building up resentment from three years of feeling neglected by Mike. It wasn't his fault that I never spoke up, but the frustration and anger began to replace the pain I felt when he wasn't around.

A year after breaking things off with Mike I met the man who would become my first husband. Sadly, I was hell bent on finding someone completely different from Mike. The new guy was classically handsome and always knew the right things to say. Our marriage lasted five years before I found his internet profile. Like an idiot, I had ignored the golden advice that is passed on to women from generation to generation. "*Once a cheater, always a cheater. Men don't change.*" He actually told me he had cheated on other girlfriends in his past but wouldn't cheat on me. *RIGHT!* (I know, I know, I just smacked my forehead really hard as I typed this). I just kept focusing on the fact this handsome, smooth, guy had chosen me. The reality was I wasn't all that special, just one of the few women who was dense enough to believe his lies.

I think I was also trying to take a break from emotional roller coaster relationships. Subconsciously, I was not strong enough for another relationship where I was deeply in love. It was much easier to be with my own stupid version of a trophy husband. He knew how to play the surface part of the good husband, how to say nice things and give attention when it was needed.

If love is heroin, I married my first husband to quit opioid love cold turkey. The relationship was just so surface and easy. We liked the same things, and we looked good together. We were very good roommates that also spent time socially. Yet, I couldn't keep my sensitivity, my predilection for reading people, down for long. One does not get over a problem by avoiding it, as it will certainly resurface.

I suspect the reason I couldn't tap into his hidden emotions, is he never allowed himself to feel them. He lived his life on the surface, covered his insecurities with lies, and didn't care enough to dig deep below the surface. So, while my sensitivity didn't read strong feelings from him, I was able to get a read on his dishonesty. I think he would have stayed in the relationship forever as it stood, a surface marriage. Yet I simply could not. My sensitivity wouldn't let me.

Throughout all of my relationships, and from the night in the tent until the present, I never stopped thinking about Chris from swim team. Little things would spark my fond memory, and I would sigh contentedly to myself and think back to that night at the team picnic. Those moments in the tent were not simply significant because of my silly, childhood crush. That night marked the start of things in my life finally turning around. I'd realized I deserved some happiness and I deserved to feel special. I was special. Chris chose me. I had value and shouldn't have to apologize for my existence.

Chapter 6

The first few "dates" with the adult Chris were really nice. We spent hours talking and laughing. Still, I constantly wondered about what was really going on between us. I would try to flirt, touch his hand, sit close to him, etc... but he would only look away nervously, thank me, and eventually leave.

For our third date Chris and I decided it might be fun to have a picnic at a local park. Even by then, I wasn't quite sure it was a date, or if we were just friends hanging out. He hadn't done more than hug me briefly since we re-united. He asked me if he needed to bring anything. I thought for a moment and mentioned I didn't have a picnic blanket. He felt confident he could come up with something. When we arrived at the picnic area he spread out a dark green army blanket, and we set up the food. As I was pulling out the sandwiches he said, "Do you remember this blanket?" I honestly didn't and said as much. He looked a bit disappointed and quietly helped me with the food. After we finished our meal, we decided to take a short hike on a trail in the woods. In a small opening in the trees we sat and rested for a few moments.

Again, Chris pulled the green blanket out of his

leather backpack and spread it on the ground.

"You sure you don't remember this?" he asked.

I shook my head apologetically.

He sighed and said, "I'm a little hurt, but it's okay."

My mind started spinning. There was no way. This couldn't be the blanket from the tent, could it? There was no way he remembered! I suddenly got very nervous. I wanted to ask him about the blanket, but for some reason I was too scared. I couldn't find the nerve to talk about it. I had told him all the yucky details of my ex-husband's infidelity, bared my soul to him, but I couldn't ask him about one silly blanket. Finally, we left the woods and went back to my apartment to talk.

I curled up on the sofa. He sat in his favorite spot on the very edge of the far-right cushion. If he had squished himself any more into the sofa arm he would have just been a head sticking out between the pillows.

I couldn't take it anymore.

"Okay," I said. "Tell me! What's up with the green blanket?"

He laughed nervously and said, "I can't believe you don't remember. That was the blanket we were sitting on in my pup tent when we kissed."

"You remember that?" I gasped.

"Remember it? I told everyone I knew. My mom,

my cousin...I thought maybe you were my girlfriend after that! I had never kissed a girl before that night."

"Oh my God, you were my first kiss too!"

He laughed and said, "I have held onto that blanket ever since, and every time I used it I thought about you. I sat on it at concerts, I used it in college—and I thought about that night each and every time."

I was stunned. STUNNED! But also, kind of turned on.

Tired of all the handshaking and pseudo-flirting that went nowhere, I finally found the courage to speak up.

"So," I said, "am I completely misreading this or are you ever going to kiss me again?"

Now it was his turn to get nervous.

He looked at his shoes and smiled, "Um, yeah, I really want to."

I inched a little closer, while he stayed pressed against the side of the couch.

"You don't have a pup tent in your car, do you?" I said. "Would it help?"

He kept his eyes on his shoelaces. "Yeah, it would help a lot."

We talked a little more about absolutely nothing. He picked nervously at the sofa cushion.

After what seemed like hours, I realized it was up to me. I finally dove in and went for it...

Chapter 7

Our wedding was beautiful. It was October 24th, 2003. Roughly two years after the sofa conversation. We had worked through some bumps along the way and it seemed like life was finally going to get easier. It felt like our entire lives were leading up to that point; the point where two damaged souls would find strength together.

As I mentioned before, this was not my first marriage. I'd already had the big, traditional wedding about six years prior to my engagement to Chris Billett. I'd been young and looking for all the wrong things when I got married the first time. I tend to be very spontaneous. There's this part of me that wants to jump into things head first and deal with the consequences later. I had lingering doubts about my first husband that existed long after the divorce. Most of the doubts were caused by his dishonesty. At first the lies were about little things. I later learned that little lies almost always accompany big lies.

Early in our relationship Chris's honesty came as a bit of a shock. I wasn't used to hearing anyone speak as frankly as he did about his feelings and thoughts on almost anything. At times, it was very hard for me to accept. I was used to hearing only what I would have wanted to hear from my first husband. If I asked Chris about an outfit or something I had cooked, he would answer with exactly what he thought, good or bad. After a few stunned reactions from me, it eventually became a comfort.

Chris never expected me to agree with him; he was just very good at expressing his point of view. There were no mysteries. I always knew exactly how he felt. If I received a compliment from Chris, I knew it was genuine. My friend Shane (who became Chris's friend too) and I would joke if you didn't want the truth, you shouldn't ask Chris. I also learned the world would not end if I was honest, and often it would actually be appreciated.

I can't know exactly what he was thinking and feeling, but I believe Chris' biggest challenge was he really wanted to be happy and contented with himself. I also think we were more alike than we ever knew. He, like me, was always looking for a place to fit and feel like himself. He also felt things so damn deeply, and as impacted as he was by successes, he was even more affected by failures. What for many of us are simply the typical difficulties of life, were so much more to him. He was in many ways allergic to failure.

Of all people, I should have known better when I

encouraged Chris to pursue a career in the restaurant business. I had been working in food service on and off, mostly on, since I was 16 years old. I knew the benefits, but I was also well aware of the downsides to this type of work. The hours are awful, the money is not always consistent, alcoholism and drug use are rampant, and serving the public is demanding. The business chews up and spits out more people than any other type of work I know.

But Chris, after a few years at the car dealership and side gig as a debt collector, was clearly unhappy with his work. He needed something new. Chris was the most incredible cook I had ever met and had been passionate about food since he was young. He watched The Food Network constantly. He rarely used recipes, and always managed to put together the most amazing and inventive meals. I loved my job as a photography teacher, and I knew firsthand how rewarding it can be to have a career you are passionate about. I was a bit blinded by my own experience when I agreed to help him jump into this line of work. The decision torments me to this day.

I suppose I always felt, most of the time unconsciously, a need to keep an eye on him at each restaurant in which he was employed. Even though I worked full time as a teacher, I also worked weekends at the restaurants where he worked. Other than a few general conflicts, mostly to do with my inability to not voice my opinion when I see something completely stupid, it was great to work with Chris.

I loved to watch him in action. He was so focused and hard working. I swelled with pride when I saw a plate of food he'd constructed. It was also fun to talk about our jobs together and be a couple who knew one another's co-workers first hand. I felt like I was part of this really great team, and I felt like those restaurants were very lucky to have the two of us. I could also support him emotionally when he needed it. Because he was so talented and good at his job, I don't think I ever truly understood how much he needed me there.

Chapter 8

"LuAnn, a car is pulling in! LU-ANN, they are writing down our license plate number."

Okay, okay, one more shot."

"LuAnn, I think they are calling someone."

Even through the sound of pelting rain I could hear the nervousness in Chris' voice as I ducked under the NO TRESPASSING sign to find a better angle. I knelt on the broken asphalt and adjusted the manual focus. The knees of most of the pants I owned were destroyed from crawling around in dirt, mud, grass, and whatever else was out there in the world. I didn't care. Some of my best shots came from the dirtiest places.

"LuAnn, *come on.*"

"Okay, I've got it."

I jumped in the car and we sped away, laughing.

"I can't wait to see how these turn out," I said. "Huge motel abandoned by the side of the road. Amazing. But why are the doors all open and the furniture intact? What's the story there?"

"I don't know, I'm just glad you didn't get us arrested."

"You know you love it."

His only answer was a half-smile. Of course, he loved it! What man doesn't love nearly getting arrested while catering to his woman's creative whims?

This was back in July of 2006. An abandoned motel north of our town by the side of an interstate highway. The kind that in its heyday probably rented rooms by the hour. Many of the doors were wide open, and a few units were black and ashy from a fire. We had noticed it months before while driving home from a concert nearby. I knew I had to go back and photograph there, and Chris knew better than to argue with me or try to talk me out of going. I was always dragging Chris to strange places for photographic exploration: nightclubs that were supposed to be closed, back alleys in Atlantic City, voodoo shops, wax museums, you name it. If it was falling apart, scary, or just plain weird, I was there, and often with my man by my side.

Because of our careers, our photography adventures required careful planning. My teaching schedule was typically Monday through Friday, late August to early June, with vacation days based mostly on holidays. Chris worked year-round which also involved covering most holidays, most evenings, and every single weekend. We didn't have much free time together, so we did our best to take advantage of the little spots of vacation time that matched up. Our life was busy, and very heavily scheduled, but it was a good life.

"What's wrong?" Chris asked.

I could hear the clanging of dishes and pans in the background.

"I just want to talk to you is all," I said. "It's nothing terrible."

The phone shook in my hand.

"So, tell me," he said.

"I really think I should tell you in person."

"Tell me now."

"Okay, um, so, yes, my period didn't come this month and I took a test. It's, well, uh, positive."

There was a very long pause and more banging in the background.

"Are you sure?"

"I read the package and a positive result is usually for sure positive. Only negative results are sometimes wrong."

Another long pause and more banging.

"Well, I guess we will have something to talk about when I get home."

We didn't have much time because I needed to leave early in the morning to travel to Philadelphia for a weekend Advanced Placement training course. It was a terrible time to have to take a class with the way my mind was spinning, and an even worse time to stop drinking caffeine. I had heard caffeine was bad for pregnant women, and more specifically their growing babies. Ironically, the very first caffeine free morning of my adult life, I would be zooming down the Schuylkill (or *Sure-kill*) expressway in Philadelphia during rush hour with only my random thoughts and a mixed CD to keep me awake.

At one point I called my mother to keep me from nodding off and waking up with my face in a guardrail.

"Just pull over and get some coffee," was her advice. She had no clue I wasn't exactly alone in the car, but I just couldn't bring myself to share the huge news over the phone.

Eventually I made it the Philadelphia Art Museum and registered. But when I settled in to the classroom I couldn't concentrate. I kept glancing around the room and wanting to yell out, "Hey, I'm pregnant! There is a baby in here! That is why you all are sipping coffee and tea and I am drinking water! I am pregnant. Me. Isn't it amazing?" Sure, women had been doing this for centuries, but it was my first time. This was a very big deal.

I should have been more focused on the conference,

but all I could think about was how it happened, when, etc.… It must have happened either right before or right after the New Year. I had a few weeks off school, and for a very short time my schedule meshed with Chris'. I could stay up late and sleep in a little, and I had the energy. I must admit we had a lot of fun during the holidays that year.

I knew that a baby would change our lives. We were used to having free time to plan guerrilla photo shoots, have friends over for dinner, or just stay in and watch movies. A baby was certainly going to change that. Yet, we had friends who had children and still seemed to find time together and do fun things. I felt like we were mature and balanced enough to make it work.

Chapter 9

It's no secret that Chris was a bit freaked out at first. We had been talking about having children, but nothing firm. My doctor had told us that since I'd been on the pill for over a decade I probably needed to be off for at least a year before there was a chance of anything happening. Chris said he was thinking maybe in another year we could start trying. We had no money saved, and we were not at all prepared financially.

When one becomes pregnant doctors refuse to see you for at least 8 weeks following conception, unless something seems wrong. I am a freaky worrier when it comes to unknown situations, and the weeks prior to the appointment killed me. When we finally heard a little heartbeat at the OBGYN, Chris gave me a big hug and a kiss. We were nervous about becoming parents, but we felt it was doable. We decided we would approach parenthood like his restaurant work, as a team.

I tried to be the perfect pregnant woman. I followed every dietary restriction, which included avoiding uncooked lunch meat, hot dogs, non-pasteurized cheese, caffeine, certain types of fish, undercooked eggs and meat, and of course, alcohol. I went to the gym three or four times a week and worked out at a safe level for pregnancy. I wore a monitor to track my heart rate. The gym staff suggested all pregnant women wear them, so they could have an accurate reading to follow.

Early in the pregnancy the expensive monitor stopped working properly. I would just be standing still or walking from one area to another, and the thing would go nuts and beep like crazy. I'd find these insanely high numbers and error messages, and the staff at the gym couldn't explain it to me. They just kept tightening the monitor belt and telling me I probably wasn't putting it on properly. I would wear it notched so tightly it dug into my ribs and it would still seem to malfunction. I had no clue something very out of the norm, from deep inside of my body, was causing the abnormal readings. This machine, which I simply thought of as a faulty, crappy, waste of money, was trying to tell me something.

At the 12 weeks mark Chris and I had an appointment with a genetic counselor and a maternal fetal medicine specialist. I was 34 years old, right at the cutoff between the average pregnancy age and advanced maternal age or AMA. The counselor was supposed to go over possible risks and potential problems, and then we would schedule another appointment with our doctor to do an early ultrasound in order to pinpoint any visible problems. We were excited and had tons of questions. When the genetic appointment ended we were somewhat surprised to find out I would have an ultrasound that morning.

Chris held my hand in the waiting area and said, "I hope everything is okay. I hope there's still a heartbeat!"

We entered the small, dark, room where I was instructed to climb on the table, lie down, and lift my shirt. Flat screen television monitors and unfamiliar machines were positioned at multiple locations in the low-lit room. As I followed the technician's instructions Chris was busy finding a place for my purse and his jacket. A moment later the scan began.

It only took about 14 seconds. Okay, so I can be an exaggerator, but it was literally 14 seconds. The technician waved the ultrasound wand over my gooey belly. We heard some flub dub sounds, and to us everything seemed just fine.

The technician smiled slightly and announced, "It's twins!"

Chris and I both laughed nervously. It had to be too soon to tell. We both figured she must use this joke with every couple.

"I never joke about that," she explained flatly. "And, well, it's triplets."

"But, but, I wasn't taking fertility treatments... and, but, I never got morning sickness... but, but...."

Apparently, I could not talk her out of her report.

Chris just stared at the screen with a blank expression. I was worried he might be permanently broken.

The doctor poked his head in with a warm smile.

"I'll be back in a few minutes to look for the fourth baby," he said.

Oh my God, he had better be kidding.

It turned out that at one time there really had been four babies. The fourth became part of something called a disappearing twin phenomenon. There was a space in one of the babies' placentas that showed where another baby had once been. Apparently, it's common for pregnancies to have a disappearing twin. Often doctors don't mention it to parents because the loss of an embryo, even very early on can be incredibly sad for many people. We already had three, so I suppose he wasn't concerned we'd be devastated by the loss of a fourth. We still had to process the fact that there were three very viable, very active little humans in my belly.

I asked if the doctor could see what the sexes were. Before he could explain that it would take a few weeks to determine gender, Chris temporarily snapped out of his coma and exclaimed, "What does it matter what the sexes are? There are three of them!"

We would eventually find our doctor to be a very warm and funny man. He was adept at relaying a wide variety of information to parents in a caring way. That same day, after a few light-hearted comments, he became serious.

"LuAnn, your pregnancy is now considered very high risk. In six weeks you will have to go on bed rest. You may not work after that time. You must stop exercising right now. For a singleton pregnancy we recommend the mother gain approximately 25 to 30 pounds. You will have to gain around 60 to 80 pounds if you can. You are a little behind on your weight gain, so you need to start eating a lot more. Your babies will most likely be born well before 40 weeks' gestation. The average is 32 weeks, and some of that may have to do with how well you gain weight, and how well you stay on the recommended bed rest. Our goal will be to get you and the babies safely to 34 weeks...Now, there is some good news and some bad news. The bad news is two of your babies share a placenta. This can put them at risk for something called twin to twin transfusion. It can be fatal for one or both babies. The good news is it appears all three babies have their own individual amniotic sacs. This will give them a bit more of an advantage because their umbilical cords cannot tangle around each other."

He explained the babies would be known as A, B, and C based on their proximity to the cervix. He then suggested a book with recommendations and instructions on how to eat, what to eat, how to prepare for multiples, information on prematurity and a variety of other topics I would soon become well versed in. His very serious tone and the definitive instructions really drove the message home: I was pregnant with triplets and I'd better start getting used to the idea.

"Should I call your parents and tell them we aren't coming over for dinner tonight?" Chris asked from deep within his comatose state.

"NO!" I said with a shaky voice. "I need my mom right now,"

We spent the first half of the drive in silence.

Then Chris spoke again, "Three college tuitions!"

"How about the fact that I have to gain 80 pounds? I can't even exercise!"

I spend a lot of time in my head to begin with, but the thoughts were zinging around like crazy. Finally, after a long, strange drive, we pulled up my parents' street.

We walked into their little house and asked them to sit down. I explained we had some news, it wasn't bad per se, but it was news.

My parents stared at us with half smiles.

"You're serious, aren't you?"

They only had to look at Chris's green face and glazed eyes to know we were, indeed, serious. Nervous excitement would be the best way to describe their reactions. Later, Chris's parents would react in a similar fashion.

The doctor had explained to us that because it was such a high-risk pregnancy, and because there is often danger to one or more of the babies, we may want to keep this news secret from most people for at least a little while. Anyone who knows me well knows that I do not possess the ability to keep a secret, especially a crazy one. I think I probably waited a total of 24 hours before I started telling people. It was just too much to keep inside.

Chapter 10

Prior to learning about the triplets, I had kept in shape and gained weight in a way that was fairly on target for a singleton pregnancy. Before long, my pregnancy began to take more of a multiple shape. The maternity outfits I didn't quite fit into previously were suddenly bursting at the seams. It was shocking for someone who was usually fairly thin and athletic in her build.

The "diet" I had been prescribed was extreme. It included a ton of high fat, high carbohydrate, and high protein foods. Premium ice cream and milkshakes were recommended. Friends and family were jealous because I could eat all this fattening food, but to be honest it became sort of a drag. I never threw up, but I tended to get a bit nauseous, and at times the mere idea of eating felt gross. For some reason, I could not eat oranges. I usually love them but when I was pregnant oranges made me gag so hard it would be years until I could even attempt to eat one again.

The worst part of the diet was the daily intake of a protein drink called Ensure. No matter what the flavor, Ensure sort of tasted to me like liquid chalk and chemicals. I found I could get it to go down better if I snacked on pretzels at the same time. The truth is I would have eaten slugs with pretzels if there was even a slight chance it would have helped my babies.

My husband and I lived on the second floor of an old building on the campus where I worked. The steps were very steep, and I was limited to one trip on the stairs a day—doctor's orders. We decided because Chris worked long hours and was rarely home, it would be better to spend my bed rest under the care of my parents at their single-story house. They were retired and home fairly often, especially because my mother had just gone through double knee replacement surgery. The plan was for my mother and I to keep one another company in our limited mobility.

I was instructed to go on bed rest at 20 weeks, but I begged to be allowed to finish the school year, which would end at the 22-week mark. The doctor tentatively agreed. My time at my parent's house would begin the day I stopped working.

It seemed to me like things were going well. At a previous ultrasound we were told with 99% certainty I was carrying two boys and a girl. We were very happy there was a mix of sexes and Chris decided it was better to have only one girl. He had this theory that boys are less emotionally competitive or something like that. I didn't care either way, I had always wanted a daughter and at least I had one.

I was only slightly uncomfortable, and Chris and I were actually looking forward to the 20-week ultrasound. It was fun to check in on the babies and see what they were up to. I should have known better to assume anything in my life would go as planned.

Our regular specialist was away from the office, and we were told his partner would be seeing us. We had never met him before, so we had no idea what to expect. The technician was unusually quiet as she scanned, but I didn't think much of it at the time. The doctor came in and ran the ultrasound wand over my belly and stared at the screen in silence. He squirted on more gel, waved the wand around again, and continued to study the image on the screen. Other than some flub dub sounds the room was painfully quiet. Chris and I looked at each other nervously.

"Well," the doctor finally said, "Babies A and B have a good amount of fluid, and things look stable for them. Unfortunately, little baby C has virtually no measurable amniotic fluid. I will be honest with you; it does not look good for her. With twins in the same placenta there are sometimes things we can do, but for a singleton in a single placenta there is nothing medically that can be done. If she dies, you will have to carry her to until it is time for A and B to be born. I just want to prepare you for the worst."

His face was stony and very solemn. Chris grabbed my hand. There were tears in my eyes, and I didn't know what to say.

The doctor also wanted to check my cervix. I don't remember if I spoke at all, and I may have just nodded. Jane came back into the room. She squirted lubricant on a very large plastic wand and guided it between my legs. An image eventually showed up on the overhead monitor. When the doctor finally spoke, it was more bad news.

"Your cervix is considerably shorter than it was at your last visit. I am going to admit you into the hospital for monitoring, and you are finished working as of today."

"But," I cried, "I only have two weeks left!"

"You are done working," he said firmly. "Your bed rest will begin immediately."

Chris' expression was blank. He was taking it all in, and not taking it well.

"Go to the lobby and tell the receptionist you are being admitted, and someone will check you into a room."

He explained this would not be a permanent stay if I didn't have strong or frequent contractions, and as long as nothing else seemed out of the ordinary. I somehow mumbled a "Thank you," and we slowly walked out to the lobby.

Chris's face was very pale.

"Do you want me to call your mom and let her know?" he asked.

I was still in shock.

"I guess you should," I said.

Chris was gone for what seemed like hours. I stared at my hands and clutched my knees. I had never been admitted to a hospital before, and certainly never spent the night in one. A few short hours earlier I'd been at school, teaching and laughing with my students. Now, suddenly I was a hospital patient and my little baby girl, who I had been so excited about, was probably not going to make it. *Why would God give me three babies only to take one away?* I didn't ask for this triplet pregnancy, but by this point I had not only accepted it, I wanted these three babies to make it very, very badly.

Chris finally returned and sat down. "I called your mom and she is on her way. I called my mom too. I told her she didn't have to come, and I will keep her posted."

"Why did he have to say the word 'die'?" I asked.

Chris shook his head and looked at his shoelaces. Chris would get quiet when he was upset. I tended to start babbling.

"I'm not giving up on her you know," I sputtered. "She is still alive and there has to be some chance she will make it."

Chris's face did not look hopeful.

A nurse finally came out to find us and to take me to my room. It was a huge space, and I would later learn these rooms were reserved for long term patients. I had no idea I would be admitted and discharged from this exact room at least three more times that summer. By the time the nurse had gone through the one million questions they ask, my mother arrived.

Tears came to my eyes as she and Chris helped me into the ugly hospital gown. The entire pregnancy was incredibly surreal, and this was just one more time where I felt like life went upside down. I was hooked up to a tocodynamometer (TOCO) monitor to check for size and frequency of contractions. I was also hooked up to these noisy, annoying inflatable things which are supposed to keep blood from clotting in your legs. I looked down at the hardware below my chest line and realized to go to the bathroom I would have to disengage all of it and reattach it afterward. By that point I was going to the bathroom every hour or two. I sighed loudly as I sank into the hospital bed. The day just seemed to keep sliding further downhill.

There is a lot a pregnant woman can try to do to give her children a good start in life. She can eat well, avoid things like alcohol, smoking, and caffeine, and follow her doctor's orders. But the reality is for the entire length of the pregnancy she will never really know if her infant or infants are going to be okay or not. Each trip to the OBGYN, fetal medicine specialist, or hospital is a search for reassurance, but there is no true reassurance, ever.

These were my children, my babies, and my maternal instinct was to fight like mad to make sure they were healthy and safe. I found out first hand there are things going on in one's uterus we have zero control over. And that may have been the hardest part. There were times I wasn't sure I was going to make it through. While some tough experiences such as standing up to bullies at work and divorcing my ex had made me stronger, I was still playing in the minor leagues. I was barely maintaining my amateur status as a woman of strength. My power of sensitivity simply had no positive application now. Instead, it simply intensified the worry and the fear.

I wasn't the only one who felt in over my head. I think sometimes these situations can be even worse for fathers—the out of control feeling. I know Chris was going through it, and being another sensitive soul, his worry and fear must have been off the charts.

Chapter 11

"LuAnn, it's time to get up. We have to leave for your doctor appointment in an hour."

I groaned. I was in my mother's scrapbooking and sewing room, which she had kindly transformed into my maternity suite. The bed was small and probably not so uncomfortable for the average human being. I, however, was 21 weeks pregnant with three babies and everything felt uncomfortable almost all the time. After I was released from the hospital my parents did their best to keep me fed and rested. I knew I was pretty lucky to have them. However, moving back in with Mom and Dad as an adult, even briefly, is never a picture-perfect experience.

I must not have spent much time with people over the age of 65 before and was soon surprised to discover even in the blazing hot summer people in this age group are constantly cold. For those of you who have never been pregnant or spent any time around pregnant women, it may be interesting to learn that our temperatures constantly fluctuate between very warm and extremely hot. The term "bun in the oven" accurately suggests this unique form of heat, which radiates from the inside out.

It's even stronger and more intense if you're carrying multiple buns. My parents chose to maintain a balmy 77 degrees in their home and did not budge from this number. No matter how much I hinted and even outright whined about my overwhelming warmth, the thermostat remained the same, and my father monitored it like the employee of the month at a nuclear power plant. Only once I could persuade my father to dip down to 75, but an hour later he clicked it right back up to 77. Not even my empty threats of lying around naked in all my pregnant glory could change his mind.

Another obstacle was the fact that I had to constantly consume as much as possible in a home whose native inhabitants ate like birds (one evening we had cheese and crackers for dinner). This situation was a little easier to fix. When I explained it was medically necessary for me to eat a lot more food, my mother started stocking more calorically dense items in her cupboards. When my father did the shopping, we had some additional bumps, because he struggled with the concept of re-stocking an item BEFORE he ran out of it. The conversations went something like this:

"LuAnn, do you need anything from the grocery store?"

"More cereal please."

The cupboard would open, followed by *shake shake shake* sounds. "You have all kinds of cereal!"

"Dad, there are five flakes in that box, and I require a few more than that to fill my bowl."

"I just don't want to end up with all kinds of boxes of half eaten cereal!"

"I'll eat it dad. I promise. By the way, I'm burning up, could you turn down the thermostat?"

My father is a retired bank president who was very successful at his job. He is stubborn, funny, and intense, almost to the point of being dramatic. He's also the most frugal man I know. He rarely buys anything unless it is absolutely necessary. If something still basically functions, he won't replace it. In college, I had a plastic bucket that I used as a trashcan. My roommate and I went through a feminist phase and covered it with stickers promoting our various causes. Once I graduated, my father commandeered our women's rights bucket for its functionality, and used it for over ten years. My conservative Republican father rinsing his rags in a bucket plastered with "SUPPORT VAGINAL PRIDE" and "FUCK THE GOVERNMENT, WOMEN TAKE CONTROL" stickers was a regular scene in their conservative neighborhood.

Most days I felt like a cat trying to hide under the

porch to have her kittens. Chris compared me to a baby steer being fattened up for a future as veal cutlets. He was all about the food metaphors. Maternity clothing soon became too small, and my wardrobe became more and more limited to men's t-shirts. I could have found larger maternity clothes but I wasn't really able to shop and it wasn't like I was going out in public.

Chris visited me as much as he could, and he called me every single night and usually a few times a day. He would update me on how things were going at work. I would update him on the pregnancy and how I was feeling. We would also discuss plans for the home that we were purchasing and other important details. He would end each call with, "I miss you. Take care and I love you."

It felt good to have my mother around me every day. She was always a super hero in my mind, and my main sidekick. As I was struggling through this phase of motherhood, it seemed appropriate for my own mother to be present. She was a calming force. When Chris was working, she attended many of my appointments with me. In some ways, it felt just as appropriate and important for her to be by my side during my high-risk pregnancy. She and I had survived a risky pregnancy together once before, when I was born, and having her around helped me hold on to hope. I needed that reminder because it wasn't always easy to be hopeful during the worst parts of my pregnancy.

The toughest four weeks were the ones when we were constantly worried about our little girl. At each ultrasound we would see the boys swimming and kicking in their fluid filled sacs. Our little peanut on the other hand was stuck in the same place each time on the right-hand corner of the screen. Her amniotic sac was stretched around her like cellophane and she could only wiggle very slightly. The blood flow to her brain and heart were good, but with each scan the doctors seemed less hopeful. I became terrified before appointments, dreading the day when she wouldn't have a heartbeat.

Sometimes strangers would approach me at the hospital and make kind hearted, positive remarks about my pregnancy. They would also ask questions. I would try to be polite but inside my mind I was screaming, "Yeah, I'm pregnant with triplets but one is going to die."

I had no reason to think about this before. There is this sort of universal belief that if a woman is pregnant, it is always this wonderful, positive, thing. The truth is, some women might not want to be pregnant, they might be carrying a child from someone they would not like to be connected to forever, or, it may be a medically problematic pregnancy. Yet strangers roll up to you with these huge smiles and try to connect to what they always seem to think is a biological miracle.

It is so hard to buzz excitedly about your pregnancy when you have been given grim and hopeless statistics. Especially to complete strangers. Because I didn't want to make people uncomfortable, I was usually good at faking it with people I didn't know. I was good at pretending I was okay, when I was far from okay.

I couldn't exactly hide my condition. At the 20-week mark I was the size of a woman who had been pregnant for eight months, instead of my four months. Like when I was a child, I just wanted to go invisible. I was not only anxious about each appointment and the fear of finding out my girl was gone, I was also worried about running into well-intentioned but nosy strangers, and whether or not I could keep from bursting into tears or punching them in the face.

My anxieties and fears were pushing up through the ceiling of my parents' house. I voiced my feelings and fears to Chris, and he said something pretty powerful to me: "You told me you weren't going to give up on her. Why are you going back on your word now?"

This moment helped me to realized it wasn't fair to her to give up just yet. Instead, I prayed even harder and thought about her all the time. Worry and fear were not doing a thing to help her. In fact, if any of my kids had inherited my sensitivity, it is possible they would absorb my crappy outlook directly in the womb. It was the first blazing sign that told me my life would no longer be about just me. My actions, my reactions, my thoughts, and feelings could have an impact on my children.

At around the 23rd week the doctor gave us a hint of both good and bad news. He explained she was still hanging on, and I was approaching the time of viability for gestating babies. Viability is the time when they can technically be born and have higher odds for survival. However, children born at 24 weeks are at very high risk for health problems, complications, and future disabilities. The odds for survival are not as high as children born later. Essentially, the longer they stay inside of the mother, the better the chances for them.

He warned us that soon we may have to make a tough decision. Do an early C-section at 24 weeks to save our little girl, but seriously risk the health of the boys, or, keep me pregnant and almost certainly risk the life of our little girl. Chris didn't want to talk about it. He kept telling me we would decide when we *had* to decide, and there was no reason to discuss it until we knew for sure. I didn't voice it, but I wanted to do anything to save my little girl.

Maybe it was my perceptiveness, maybe my emotional state, but both choices seemed wrong, out of the question, and impossible. I was determined to find a way for all three to survive and be healthy. This moment marked one of the first strong appearances of Sensitivity Girl, the super hero. Yes, I was emotional, but my anger and uncompromising resolution triggered a power I'd never known. Dammit, these babies were all going to make it because they were mine, they were part of me, and I loved them all. It wasn't just about me anymore.

At the 24 week ultrasound the tech started the usual scan. I was always nervous at the scans but this one really freaked me out. It was time. We would have to decide our little girl's fate.

The technician who often did our scans was quiet as she waved the wand over our baby C. Then she smiled slightly and whispered, "She has fluid."

Chris and I looked at each other, and then back at the screen.

"I'll go get the doctor," she said.

The doctor came in and sat down beside my head. He waved the wand over the right-hand side of my huge belly and examined the screen. "Yep, baby C has fluid. Not a ton, but much more than she did before, and she can move. She is quite a bit smaller than her brothers, but it doesn't always indicate a problem."

"Does this mean she's going to be okay?"

"I've seen this maybe one other time in my entire career. It just doesn't happen. We still have to keep an eye on things, but as of today it looks like a miracle."

Chris smiled nervously. He was never great at accepting good news. It always seemed to take him by surprise. "So, we don't have to make any major decisions today?" he asked, his voice tinged with relief.

"No decisions today, and LuAnn's cervix looks good, so you can go home until the next ultrasound."

The next six weeks were filled with more appointments, more overnight visits to the hospital, and more discomfort. With each scan baby C seemed to be swimming in increasingly higher levels of fluid. There were even times she had more fluid around her than her brothers. We were relieved, but we also knew the babies were not out of the woods by a long shot. There was still a mountain of things that could go wrong for any of them, so I continued to follow the doctor's orders, and I kept on praying.

Meanwhile, I was getting increasingly tired. Taking a shower was exhausting. Afterward I would have to sit down and rest as though I had run around the block five times. I stopped putting on makeup and stopped drying my hair with a hairdryer. It was all just too tiring. Breathing had become difficult, and I felt at times like someone was sitting on my chest. I only wore sandals because putting on socks was too hard. I had read that a triplet pregnancy can be tough for a woman who has never been pregnant before because her body is just not prepared for it. I doubt anything could have really prepared me for the physical and emotional reality of growing three children at once.

At each appointment, I would be hooked up to fetal monitors and a TOCO machine for at least a half an hour. This was to monitor for contractions and to see how the babies were handling them by checking heart rates. I'd had some contractions previously and been hospitalized to receive steroid shots for the babies' lungs in case of an early labor. I was also put on an oral medication called Procardia to help hold off the contractions. The goal was to keep me pregnant as long as possible. When a woman is pregnant with multiple babies, her body tends to think she is ready to give birth well before 40 weeks. The cervix shortens early, and contractions of any kind can be dangerous. Another danger is pre-eclampsia. This is a condition which causes high blood pressure, kidney problems and sometimes death. My blood pressure was closely monitored. I had never had high blood pressure prior to my pregnancy but because of the strain on my body my blood pressure was often on the high side.

I had between two to four appointments at the Lancaster General Women and Babies Hospital every week. It was tiring traveling back and forth to the hospital, which was about 20 minutes from my parents' home. I tried to make the best of each visit by doing some people watching, and I could observe many different pregnancy types. I saw happy couples waiting nervously for appointments, but I also saw many single and young mothers. Also, I witnessed quite a few pregnant women, IV poles in hand, smoking cigarettes outside of the facility. It always made me sad and a little angry.

Sometimes I ended up more isolated in the triage area of the hospital. In this section patients must wait on very tall skinny adjustable tables. More like glorified room service carts than beds. The rooms are tiny, bright, and noisy. It was best when the time spent in triage was short. One of the triage visits was especially bad. I was left for what seemed like hours on bed/table/cart contraption and hooked up to monitors so a decision could be made as to whether or not I should be admitted. As I lay on the slab feeling like I could roll off of it at any moment, I heard loud noises out in the hall. There was yelling and banging, and I heard a nurse say something about calling the police. All I could picture was an angry father, full of grief over the loss of his child or his wife, running around and gunning down every pregnant woman he could find.

Most of the time I try to imagine if I were in a violent situation I would protect myself with the strength and agility of Laura Croft or Trinity from the Matrix. Sensitivity does not necessary cause one to be wimp. I, for one, have a strong sense of physical self-preservation. While I've never been in a physical fight, I've always felt, if the occasion arose, I could kick some serious ass.

Emotions can be incredibly painful for me. Physical pain on the other hand is not something I'm all that afraid of. Most of the time, if given the option, I'd choose a slap on the face over someone yelling awful things at me. The idea of standing up for myself physically was never as scary as standing up for myself emotionally.

On that day however, I was feeling more like Mama Cass or Shamu the Killer Whale. I didn't even have a ham sandwich or frozen fish to throw at an attacker. I looked around the room. It was tiny, and I was huge. The door didn't have a lock. Not only could I not fight back, I couldn't even hide. I simply had to sit nervously on my little table and wait. Minutes passed, but it felt like hours, and eventually a nurse came in to discharge me. She acted like all was perfectly normal. Like nothing dangerous had happened.

I found out later it was an angry father, and he was upset because he was not permitted to see his pregnant girlfriend. He had been physically abusive to her, and she had been admitted to the hospital for her own protection. The security staff had taken care of it, but even though I was relieved to be safe, my heart went out to the woman. What kind of man abuses the mother of his child?

Chapter 12

At around 30 weeks things were not looking so good during my regular monitoring. I was having contractions and not feeling them. My blood pressure was high, and my cervix was short. The Maternal Fetal Medicine specialist delivered the news: I was to be admitted to the hospital, and I was most likely going to remain there until I delivered. He was concerned about pre-eclampsia. The medication I had been taking to slow down contractions was possibly masking signs of this condition. He wanted more constant and close monitoring.

I felt a bit defeated, but I was also tired of traveling back and forth from my parent's house to appointments. I wasn't too upset with the idea of just staying in the hospital. Going into labor would be far less scary there than at my parent's house in the middle of the night. I literally had nightmares about my parents scrambling around in the dark, and me finally just giving birth on their sofa because my father had taken too long to put on his shoes.

Once I got settled into my room, the same one that I had stayed in a few times before, I was exhausted. I was nervous as it was still a bit early for the babies to be born, but I was also pretty ready for the experience to be over. Once again, they hooked me up to a TOCO monitor and fetal monitors. The doctors and nurses kept a close eye on the pieces of paper that flowed out of the main printer. They monitored me for a few days and the results seemed normal. At least to me. But what the hell did I know?

A few days into my stay a young doctor came in and explained that the medical staff suspected I had pre-eclampsia and they wanted to take me off of the Procardia, the drug holding off the contractions. I immediately became very frightened and asked if my regular doctor knew about this. He told me the specialist would come in to see me to explain things. When he left me alone, my mind started racing. Tears flowed down my cheeks. Was this really the right thing to do? I thought the goal was to keep me from going into labor? Wasn't it too early? Would the babies have to spend a ton of time in the NICU? Was baby C big enough or strong enough for all of this?

The next morning my doctor and the maternal specialist came into my room and explained what was going on. I had two rounds of steroid shots for the babies' lungs. At this point my health was quite possibly in more danger than theirs, so it really was best to just let nature take its course. I asked how long it would be before I would go into labor. The specialist explained it was hard to predict, but probably at least a few days. I called Chris right away and with a shaky voice I updated him on the situation. What I had planned on and hoped for and prayed about was going to happen soon, and I was filled with the wildest mix of emotions I had ever experienced.

Chapter 13

"Passport, Bitte!"

The lights in the ancient, cramped train car flashed on overhead. It was blinding, but through my squinted eyes I made out the fuzzy shape of a German border guard. Hands shaking, I reached for my passport in the secret pocket of my cargo pants. I handed the man my documents. He collected the papers and passport books from the five other passengers in my compartment and walked out into the hall. At 28 years old this was the most frightening experience of my life, and it was getting worse by the moment. *What was I thinking traveling alone from Germany to Poland on a night train? No one really had any idea where I was, and if something happened to me, who would know? And now my passport is in the hands of a stranger, and I don't know where he went.*

I'm not afraid of the unknown as it pertains to places and experiences. I love to go to places I've never been. I generally know how to protect myself and I am pretty smart and careful. Being sensitive does not seem to cause a fear of the unknown in me. I am actually pretty scrappy in most situations.

My fears tended to relate more in not trusting

others to take care of me. Memories from times when I needed help and didn't get it, combined with not wanting to inconvenience other people, made it nearly impossible to reach out for help. So, for the longest time I tried my best not to get into any situations where I would end up relying on others.

It had become second nature to avoid needing other people in more than a surface way. So, to suddenly realize I was completely isolated, alone, and with no means of communication, was scary as hell. I not only had no one I could rely on, I wasn't one hundred percent sure I could rely on myself if something went horribly wrong. The year 2001 does not seem that long ago, but communication wise, it felt like I was traveling in the dark ages. Back then, cell phone service was not transferable from continent to continent like it is today. Wifi was not really a thing yet. My parents knew my itinerary, but I'd left Germany a day early so no one realized I had changed my plans.

The sun came up as the train pulled into Warsaw. Somehow, with the three Polish words I memorized prior to the trip, I was able to take a taxi and find a hotel. The hotel was clean but slightly scary. The door of my room had clearly been kicked in at one point, and the lock hastily replaced. I did not know enough of the language to complain, so I jimmied a chair under the door handle and "slept" with the lights on. The next morning, I took a cab to the Warsaw airport and met my friends from home, including my bestie, Shane. I leapt into Shane's arms like the wife of a long-lost sailor.

The rest of my trip was quite different from the first leg. We taught English at a summer camp near Krakow. We ate Polish food, learned local customs, and got to know the teenagers at the camp. We traveled all over Poland on weekends and through a hosted trip at the end of our time there. I not only learned about a country I had almost zero knowledge of previously, but I learned that sometimes it was better to have others around you when things were scary or new. This didn't mean I'd completely resolved my fears about totally relying on other people.

Years later, when I realized that the births of my three children were inevitable and quickly approaching, a similar fear returned. I felt completely out of my element. This was supposed to be one of the most significant, beautiful moments in my life, but it felt more like I was on a speeding train. Fears about medical mistakes, blood, anesthesia, surgery, life, death, EVERYTHING ran through my head. It is appropriate to say I was paralyzed by fear because in all honesty, by that point, the pregnancy had already paralyzed me.

I kept telling myself that women had been doing this for hundreds of years and the odds were in my favor that it would work out. The other side of the argument, though, was the fact that I had never done this before, and I learn by *doing*. I like to try things out a few times before doing it for real, like practicing for a driving test or taking music lessons before performing in a recital. With pregnancy, there is no run through, no dress rehearsal. Too bad if you're a slow learner.

It was 4 A.M. July 22nd, 2007, and I had actually been sleeping well for about two hours. Chris had visited after work and left my hospital room at around 2 A.M. to go home and get some rest before he had to be at work the next day. I went to the bathroom just like I had millions of times during my pregnancy. The wetness seemed out of the ordinary, though, and the pains were a little strange. I figured it was probably nothing, but it may be a good idea to report it to the night nurse. I lay back on the bed and buzzed the call button. I described my concerns and the nurse brought in this little swab and dabbed it at the wetness. The swab changed color. She said, "Are you ready to meet your babies?"

Of course, I was ready and excited to meet them in person and hear their little cries.

On the other hand, I was NOT ready at all. I really just wanted to go back to sleep and worry about it all the next day. What ever happened to practicing medicine? It seemed like everyone around me insisted on doing things in more of a final exam manner.

What she should have asked was "Are you ready to have a needle stabbed into your spine, get strapped down to a table under a light as bright as the sun, and have your belly cut in half? Are you ready to have your organs shuffled around while a doctor reaches into your abdomen up to his elbow and pulls out your babies?"

No, I wasn't ready. For such an experience, there might not be any such thing as *ready*. It was like being back on that night train wondering what the hell I got myself into.

Instead of laying all of that on her I just asked if I should call my husband. The nurse smiled and nodded. A sleepy Chris answered the phone. He had only been home for about an hour and half.

"Honey, I uh, I think it is time. My water broke." In a confused and dazed voice, he asked if he had time for a shower. Not really thinking straight I said, "Sure, it can't be happening right this instant."

Next, I called my parents and told them the same thing. I hung up the phone. The lights came on in my room, which was suddenly filled with people. "The doctor on duty is Doctor F, and he is on his way." I relaxed a little. He was our favorite doctor. He had this great, weird sense of humor Chris and I both loved, and he always made me feel comfortable. He spoke German, rode a motorcycle and wore a helmet that made him look like a storm trooper from Star Wars. To my whacked-out sense of logic, these were all signs of incredible competence.

"What size is your husband?" Suddenly, that was the hardest question that anyone had ever asked me. My mind spun, *he wears a size large, but then again, he isn't a large person. Maybe he is really a medium, but his clothing is size large. I mean he isn't like, a big guy, he is more on the medium size and hospital things run on the larger size, right?*

I babbled all of this at the nurse, who looked at me like maybe I wasn't really in the right place for hard questions. She shrugged and told me she would find something that seemed right. At this time, I realized this birth thing really was probably happening and there was no turning back. They were finding outfits for Chris and they changed me into a different hospital gown. Everyone was working really fast and all I could do was lay back and blink.

Dr. F strolled into the room in jeans and a t-shirt, sipping an iced tea and looking rested. He must get a lot of middle of the night calls. It didn't seem to faze him. His relaxed attitude comforted me.

"How far did your husband have to travel?" he said. "I'm here before he is!"

"I told him he could take a shower before he drove in."

The doctor's eyebrows raised, and I suddenly wondered if I'd made a mistake. He wouldn't miss this, would he? A few minutes later Chris walked into the room, and I relaxed a little. He had time to give me a quick peck on the cheek before the nurses shoved his turquoise scrubs into his arms and instructed him to change. He walked out of the bathroom tugging on his pants and announced that these must have been chosen based on his pre-pregnancy weight.

Moments later my parents walked in and my mother had tears in her eyes.

"I saw the three bassinets in the hallway." she cried behind a smile. I smiled back but inside the fear washed over me again.

"What is taking so long?" one of the nurses mumbled.

"We need one more oxygen tank and they had to drive it in from the General downtown."

Taking So Long. I thought to myself. *This whole*

experience was going pretty damn fast for me. I honestly wouldn't mind things slowing down just a bit. Perhaps we could just sit around and chat with Doctor F about motorcycles or Star Wars or something. I'm not ready for this.

A minute or two later they'd unlocked my bed and were pushing me down the hall.

"You sit here, Dad," the nurse told Chris, pointing to a hard chair in the hallway outside the surgical suite. Chris sat down obediently. He had a nervous look in his eye. I was wheeled into the brightest room I'd ever seen and instructed to sit on the edge of the surgical table. I met the anesthesiologist, who explained the type of spinal injection they were giving me and what it would do. I can't really tell you exactly what he said. All I remember was I had to lean forward and not move. I stared at my swollen feet dangling over the cold, tile floor, and prayed like mad. I felt a little pinch in the middle of my back and that was it. The nurses helped me to lie back on the table, and someone went into the hall to get Chris. The room was full of people in blue surgical masks, and if I saw any of them later in the hospital or on the street, I wouldn't be able to tell you if they were there or not.

A paper curtain was crudely hung in front of my face. My arms were strapped down. I kept praying, *please don't let the flimsy blue paper fall down.* I didn't want to see what was going on below. I had watched a lot of C-sections on Discovery Health Channel, but I didn't really want to picture it happening to me. I only wanted to see my babies. No blood. No guts.

Chris eagerly peeked over the curtain. "Is it okay if I watch?"

He stepped closer to the end of the table. I felt some tugging on my stomach and kept telling myself the doctor was just looking for a good place to make an incision, and wasn't actually anywhere close to cutting, reaching in, or pulling out babies.

After a short time, I felt a big tug, and something come out from below. I felt a few pounds lighter. I also heard a beautiful, audible cry from behind the sheet. "Baby A is out and it's a boy!" Dr. F quickly held him above the sheet. I felt one-third relieved. Less than a minute later I felt another tug, a bit lighter, and I heard another cry. "Baby B is out and it's a boy!" I was given another quick peek from above the curtain. Thirty seconds later I felt some stronger tugs and I heard a one last beautiful little cry. "Baby C is out and it's a girl!" One quick look over the curtain as my little peanut was passed to the Neonatologist.

The bassinets were parked on my right and I could watch the doctors and nurses examining my babies. Baby girl C was closest to me, and I noticed a doctor who seemed really focused on her. He was vigorously rubbing her chest and inflating and deflating a little blue bag over her mouth. I watched nervously until Dr. F peeked over the curtain and got my attention.

Eventually, as I was being sewn up, the nurses held out each little tiny swaddled baby for me to kiss before my children were wheeled away to the NICU. Chris was instructed to follow. I wasn't sure what had happened with baby C, but It seemed she was okay now, so I felt a little better. Sadly, with my family gone I suddenly felt lonely in a room full of people. My job was finished. I felt like a vessel and not a person. It was 5:30A.M. and everything had happened so quickly.

I was wheeled into a recovery area where I tried to mentally recuperate from what I had just experienced. My legs were still a bit frozen from the spinal. It was very early in the morning and I was the only one in the recovery suite. For quite some time there weren't even nurses there. I felt emptier than I had in a long time. For months, I hadn't had a moment alone. Not only was I rarely left alone in case I needed something or in case of an emergency, but I'd had three people living inside of me. In essentially one hour's time I went from a specialized container for incredibly fragile and important items, to an empty, discarded wrapper. It may sound dramatic, but the shift in my job description felt that distinctive.

Finally, Chris returned from the NICU, chattering excitedly about what he had just seen. "Baby A was still partially inside of you when he started to cry. The babies are being settled into the NICU, but things look pretty good. Baby C had a rough start and she had to be revived but I think she's going to be okay. I saw a bunch of your internal organs. When the doctor cut into you a big spray of fluid shot across the room and hit the wall!"

I smiled. At least Chris had enjoyed himself. I, on the other hand was feeling like a businessman in a foreign country who had awakened with half his vital organs harvested.

Chris went out to the hallway to get my mother, so she could come and see me. She was buzzing, too. She and my father had gotten to see the babies as they were taken to the Neonatal unit, and she told me how beautiful they were. The nurse in the recovery area let me know I did a good job, and that I seemed to be recovering well. I was able to wiggle my leg and that was a good sign. She also told me I would probably be in some pain when the spinal wore off. Apparently, the hard part was not completely over. My mom smiled and said, "You're a mom now," in a really proud voice which gave me some needed strength. I was still important. I still had a job to do.

Eventually, I was wheeled out of the recovery area and put on a hospital bed and wheeled into the NICU.

"Are you ready to see them?" a kind nurse said.

I smiled weakly as I was pushed into a small room called a pod. I was excited to see them again, but I was nervous. I knew they would be small and hooked up to machines which frightened me a bit. She wheeled me over to baby A first. From my bed I could see him, and I was struck by how beautiful he was. I had never had a baby before, so I didn't have anything to compare it to, but I thought he was just perfect.

Next, I was wheeled to another pod to meet baby B. I couldn't believe his big eyes and perfect little hands and feet. The last baby for me to see was baby C. My little miracle girl. She was so tiny and so amazing. I just couldn't believe she was actually alive. Even through the tubes and wires, each baby was flawless in my eyes.

There were nurses there to update me on how each one was doing, but for the life of me I can't remember what any of them said. This might sound strange but at the moment each of them was born, and when I heard each of them cry, I knew deep down in my heart all three were going to be just fine. My sensitivity was working in my favor at that time. I knew these kids were going to be with me for the long haul.

In the coming weeks, the nurses would occasionally comment on my attitude... How the alarms on the machines that monitored their vital signs never seemed to bother me. How the slow progress of a neo-natal stay never seemed to worry me. How different I seemed from most neo-natal unit moms.

The reason was actually pretty simple. Instead of reading their thoughts and feelings, I was able to connect with my babies in an even deeper way. I knew they were strong. I knew they were fighters like me. I absolutely knew they were going to make it through the coming days and weeks. I only needed to see them and hear them to understand this truth with incredible clarity. The super part of my super power was finally kicking in.

I don't, however, think it was the same for Chris.

Chapter 14

A few hours after the birth of my children there was a knock on my hospital room door. Instead of a doctor, nurse, or visitor, a young woman walked in wearing a long skirt, even longer hair, and an enormous smile. I was not smiling. I was in a haze of pain and exhaustion. The blur of perkiness told me she was the lactation consultant and was there to give me a breast pump lesson.

I peered at this sweet, bubbling, girl from under my covers and realized she was completely serious.

"Sure," I groaned

She spent the next several minutes explaining how a breast pump worked.

"Now I would like you to try it."

I stared at her. She had demonstrated, very clearly, the proper technique for using this machine, which involved the user assuming a hunched over body position. Like a very tight sit up or abdominal crunch. Only a few short hours before, I had been practically sawed in half and no amount of morphine was letting me forget it. Moving even two inches triggered searing pain. I was usually a good sport and a tough cookie, and I hated to disappoint those whose intentions were so good, but I had to say, "no way," it wasn't happening.

She looked at me with a mixture of shock and shame.

"You know, it is best to start pumping right away to get your milk supply started."

I told her, "It isn't happening today. You are going to need to come back tomorrow." I knew the babies were only on IV fluids at that time and that the nurses weren't even close to starting them on breast milk. The consultant and my boobs would just have to be patient.

A few hours later a big, burly nurse came into the room. She immediately started buzzing around and fixing my IV and inspecting my catheter bag.

"Who has been taking care of you? Your IV is falling out and your catheter bag is the fullest I've ever seen."

I sighed, I didn't really care about those things and had been sort of happy to be left alone. She moved me over a few inches to change a pad under my bottom. I almost punched her, the pain was so intense.

"It's time to take out this catheter anyway and get you up to the bathroom."

Tears came to my eyes. "I'm not ready to go get up and go the bathroom," I whined.

Unfortunately, this nurse was not the pushover that the lactation lady was, and she went into the hall to get another nurse to help her. Together they pulled me to a sitting position on the side of the bed, and one of them pulled out the catheter. The pain was so strong it made me dizzy. Chris came into the room around that time and the nurses got him to join them in support of my toilet efforts. All three of them dragged me into the bathroom and sat me on the toilet, with my head spinning from nausea and pain, and... nothing. Audience or not I tried, I really did, but nothing was coming out.

"That's okay," the burly nurse assured me. "We will just try again in an hour or two." They put me back in bed, which involved more crippling pain, and I lay there dreading their next visit.

Chris updated me on the babies. He was proud and excited, but also deeply concerned. I had done a lot of research on multiples and on prematurity and had some idea of what medical conditions were common and what types of bumps to expect. He had been busy working and was not nearly as prepared. Baby A was 3lbs 8ozs, Baby B was 3 lbs 12 oz, and Baby C was 2 lbs 6 oz. They were small, but I knew that these weights were not unusual for multiples. I knew that they would need supplemental oxygen, and they did. I also knew they could have holes in their hearts that are supposed to close at birth but often don't in preemies. They each suffered from this condition and were receiving medication to correct it. Jaundice is also common, and each baby was showing signs of this as well. But once again, I simply knew in my heart that they were going to be okay.

Chris stayed for a while, but eventually he went home to rest. It had been a crazy day for him as well and he needed sleep.

Early the next morning I was feeling a bit better and Chris returned to help me to the NICU. He instructed me on how to wash my hands before wheeling me to the first pod to visit Baby A. The nurse gave us a cheerful update and congratulated me on making it to 31 weeks' gestation. I smiled weakly. I was actually pretty upset with myself for not making it to 34 weeks. I was sad to see how small my babies were, and I wondered inwardly if maybe I could have made it longer. Maybe I didn't really have preeclampsia, and I could have hung in there. It was really too late to think such things, but it is hard not to when your babies are in incubators struggling for life.

Next, Chris wheeled me to baby B's side. He was wearing little sunglasses and a diaper and sleeping under a photo therapy light. The light hurt my eyes and I was glad to be sitting in the wheelchair. In the corner of the room I saw that Baby C was also under a similar light and wearing the little foam glasses. Even in this dizzying blue light they looked so beautiful to me. These early memories are hazy. Not only was I recovering from major surgery for the first time in my life, but I was also a bit overwhelmed by the whole experience. Chris escorted in a sea of visitors to the Neonatal Unit, but only one person could visit at a time. Those waiting were often stuck in my hospital room staring awkwardly at me while I tried to sip some chicken broth and make small talk.

After everyone left we decided that it was time to talk seriously about names. From the time we found out that we were having two boys and a girl Chris was fixated on calling them Bo, Luke, and Daisy. You know, from the Dukes of Hazard. To this day I am still not completely convinced he was kidding about that, but I refused. Daisy was completely out of the question. I had no desire for my daughter to have a name that is more suited to an exotic dancer than the C.E.O of a company.

"It would be so cute." Chris would say.

"Cute is not part of my criteria for naming children," I would shout firmly.

I did mention that Gabrielle might be a good name. It means strength from God which we both felt suited her. Annika would be her middle name after Chris's grandmother. I brought up Charles, my grandfather's name, with the idea that we could call him Charlie. Chris loved the name as Charlie and the Chocolate factory was his favorite book as a child. He also loved that I wanted to use Michael, his cousin and uncle's name as his middle name. That would give him the same initials as Chris. I already knew which boy Charlie would be. Baby B already seemed to be the more relaxed and laid back of the two boys.

Our other boy was harder to name. I had a few of those baby name books and one day in my hospital room we started brainstorming with my sister-in-law and my niece about the third name. We threw around a ton of possibilities, but nothing seemed quite right.

Suddenly, Chris said, "What about Anthony William?"

William is my father's name and Anthony is the name of one of our favorite chefs.

"I love it," I said, "Baby A will be Anthony William."

Inside, I was able to relax. No Bo, Luke, or Daisy.

Eventually, my pain lessened, and I was able to start using the breast pump. I was starting to feel like a real person again. The five days at the hospital were mostly spent pumping, visiting the babies, taking pain killers, signing forms, and sleeping. The time to go home was inching closer and I was feeling anxious about it. I didn't want to leave my babies. I knew before they were even born that I would be going home without them, but even though I felt like I was prepared, I wasn't. The idea of leaving them behind was devastating.

Chapter 15

"Kevin does not want to see his parents right now. He only wants to talk to LuAnn."

I was 11 years old and sitting in the atrium of the mental and behavioral health ward of a local hospital. I was dressed in my lavender Sunday school-dress, white knee socks, black patent shoes, and felt completely out of place. I could think of about a million other places I would rather be. I nodded slowly at my brother's case worker, and followed her through a set of double doors.

The area looked like the hallway of an average hospital ward. There were rooms to my left and a nurse's station. People who looked like doctors and medical staff buzzed around the desk. In the middle of the hallway, we stopped in front of a room with an open door. The caseworker knocked on the door frame and led me in. My brother was sitting on the bed in gray sweatpants and a dark sweatshirt. His hair was wild, and he looked very upset.

"I'll be back in about ten or fifteen minutes okay?"

Neither of us said anything to the lady, and she left the room. I felt very uncomfortable and simply stood awkwardly near the bed.

"Welcome to my new home!" Kevin said, his voice dripping with sarcasm and anger. "You know, I am in the worst place possible. They think I'm crazy. I could do anything to you, and no one could do a thing about it. This is worse than jail. Isn't that great?"

He looked directly at me with wild eyes.

I inched a little closer to the door. I didn't say a word, and my eyes darted around the room. *Was there a clock in here? When is that stupid lady coming back?* He wasn't serious, was he? He wouldn't try to hurt me in here, would he? How could my parents have let me come in alone?

The previous day I had been swimming with my friends at the local pool. I heard my name called over the loudspeaker system and pulled myself out of the water. My sister stood by the exit to the parking lot.

"Get your stuff. Mom and Dad asked me to pick you up. We're going to the Williams family's house for a while. There is a problem with Kevin, and we can't go home."

"But I only have my bathing suit and some shorts," I whined in a low voice. "Linda, I don't even have *underwear* in my bag."

"We can't go home. Just get your stuff, and we will figure things out when we get to their house."

I found out later that there had been a big blowup with my brother. The police had to be called, and he ran away from my parents. They said he might try to come back to the house. He was out of control in their opinion. Later that night they found him and admitted him into the psychiatric ward of a local hospital. It would be about two or three long years of similar incidents until things finally got better for Kevin and my family. This time in my life was a series of nightmares, but I can only imagine what kind of hell my brother went through. He was only three years older than me.

While my sensitivity made the experiences with Kevin difficult for me as a kid, there was a benefit. I always knew his anger and strong emotions had little to do with me. I also knew it wasn't his fault. I could recognize, with certainty, he was a good guy who had been given a raw deal.

My father was hard on me as his only biological child. He was hard on my brother as his only son. He would get very angry at Kevin for what seemed to me like really small things: a broken fishing lure, muddy shoes, etc... My father not only punished him with words, he physically punished him. Even as a small child I remember thinking, "Wow, that is extreme," when my father was disciplining my brother.

It had to be hard for Kevin. To have to deal with the many confusing feelings about adoption, and then to have his father treat him so harshly. Kevin was actually a sweet and easy young kid, so I think the extremes in discipline had to have hurt him deeply. After so many years of both of us receiving negative attention the pain pushed me deeper inside of myself, and Kevin's pain came out as rage. It took years, but eventually he was able to get back on track, and my brother would eventually become one of my biggest and best super hero sidekicks.

Yet at this point in my life, more than 25 years later, the fear and confusion I had felt as a helpless kid in the hospital was back. This time it wasn't my brother scaring me, it was my husband.

While I was still in the hospital, the babies a little over 1 day old, Chris called me to complain: "You tricked me into buying this house, and now it is falling apart! The sink in the bathroom doesn't work and the washer only washes clothes on hot. You need to do something about this."

I babbled something about still being the hospital, and he hung up. I stared at the phone in my hand and didn't know what to think. I'd never heard him talk like that before.

Chris and I had bought a house and he moved in to

it at the beginning of July, 22 days prior to the children being born, and I hadn't even seen the house since the settlement date. I just didn't know what to expect. In some ways I was excited, but I was also nervous about returning to my "regular" life post pregnancy. In the hospital, I only had to worry about pumping milk every few hours and visiting babies. Coming home would suddenly add a pile of new things to deal with. Apparently, these things were already getting to Chris.

After work that night he came to visit. He was still upset. He slumped into a chair and sighed. "The glass that covered my grandmother's end tables is missing from the storage room at your school. I think it was stolen. You need to call someone at the school and get it back or have the school replace it."

"Chris, you know that the storage area isn't locked," I said, "and they are just going to tell me that we put things there at our own risk. It is only glass. I'll replace it later."

"That is bullshit. That glass has been in my family for two generations and is from my grandparents. You better call the school, and they better replace the glass, or I'm calling the police."

"Chris, I still work there. I can't do that!"

"Well, you don't have a choice."

And with that he stormed out of the room.

I stared at the door as tears rolled down my cheeks. I'd just given birth to his three children. What was going on? Wasn't he supposed to be buying me gifts and fluffing my pillow? Instead I was being threatened.

From that day on, most of my conversations with Chris involved some similar insanity. He told me he had to work on the day I would be released from the hospital, and he wouldn't be able to drive me home. Luckily my mother was available and willing to help, but I was starting to feel like something was very, very wrong.

Chapter 16

Early Fall 1991.

I was in the dorm building of the Manhattan campus of Pace University. My friend Chrisa and her boyfriend gave me hugs and left me alone in my new room. I was 18 years old and away at college. The campus of Pace University that I had chosen was in downtown New York city. My parents were okay with my choice but made it clear they were not going to move me in or out of a dorm room in New York City. It was the first time in my life I had made a major change that was going to greatly impact my future. It was also the first time that I was doing something like this completely on my own.

I picked up the note that my new roommate left me and read it again:

"Hi! My name is Marilee, I'm a senior, and I'm your roommate. I'm going to be away for the weekend in New Jersey, so I will see you on Monday. We can talk about how to arrange the room when we meet. Don't steal any of my stuff!"

I looked around the room and suddenly felt nervous and alone. It was my first night in New York City, and I didn't know what to do. A resident assistant I'd met earlier in the elevator had invited me to play Pictionary that evening with some other new students, but I sort of blew him off. Board games with a bunch of other college freshmen my first night in the big city seemed like a joke. As I sat in my empty room I started to regret my arrogance.

Later in the hall I met two potentially cool people. Lerna was from New York and her parents were Armenian. Ni'ati was from New Jersey and her parents were from India. They both seemed super exotic to me. My family had been in the United States since the 1700's. I quickly learned in New York, when someone asks you where you are from, they mean your cultural background, your home country. By New York city standards I was super normal. Yet, no one made me feel lame when I answered Pennsylvania. More importantly, no one cared who my family was. I could just be 100% me, no excess baggage.

Lerna just happened to have a close cousin who was a promoter for a club called Rex. On Tuesday's we would stroll up to the head of a block long queue in front of the club, kiss Curtis on the cheek and walk right in. We didn't even need to be on his guest list. Our theory was, if we had to pay to get in, it wasn't worth going. On almost every other night of the week Curtis would put us on the list of other great clubs like China club, Limelight, Palladium, and so many others that I can't even remember all the names. I was this 18-year-old from the middle of nowhere and suddenly I was dancing at the same clubs as celebrities and models. It wasn't like at home where most people had known me my entire life, where no matter what I did, I suffered from a pre-conceived identity. In New York, I not only could be anyone I wanted to be, I felt special.

It didn't last. The club scene had a collective short-term memory problem. If a "member" of a club was off the scene for the summer, or even for a week in some cases, they would have needed to re-establish themselves. Re-connect with the right people. Get back on the lists. I may have gotten into the scene without trying, but to stay in it, I would need apply intense effort, full time. I was too sensitive to play such a shallow, constantly changing social game.

As Chris and I drove home from the hospital I felt like I had during my time in New York. I was starting an exciting new life, with a husband and three kids and a brand-new home. I had gone away a few months, to take my bedrest and deliver the children, only to come back on the scene and discover the rules of the game had changed. Chris no longer seemed to recognize me, and I certainly didn't recognize him. It hadn't been a surprise to learn NYC clubs were so fickle. It was, however, a shock to learn my marriage could change so dramatically in such a short time.

My mother and Chris's mother helped me settle into the house, and I rested until Chris came home from work. Instead of giving me a huge hug and a welcome to our home, I was given a list of rules: which doors to keep locked, which lights to turn off, and that I was never supposed to leave the dog home alone. I was feeling weak and vulnerable, so I just nodded in agreement to everything. I thought I would feel a little better once he laid down beside me. We hadn't slept together in months and I was looking forward to sharing the bed with him. Sadly, an hour or two later I was in trouble again.

"I can't sleep with you snoring, like that. Can't you turn over or something?"

I mumbled a "sorry" and turned over on my side, which was still a bit painful. An hour later he woke me up again.

"You are still snoring, and I can't sleep."

"I'm sorry, I'm trying not to. I didn't realize I was doing it."

He grabbed his pillow in a huff and said, "I'm going downstairs." He stormed out of the room, and that would be the last time he shared a bed with me.

I stared at the door and cried. *What the hell was going on? Who was this person?* The entire time I was pregnant Chris had called me every single night. He always closed the conversation with a "take care and I love you." I was completely in shock and had no idea what to do about this man who had replaced him.

The next morning, I thought maybe he would apologize, but instead I was met with more hostility. I wasn't permitted to drive for a few weeks and Chris had also crashed my Mitsubishi a few weeks before. At the time, he had promised to buy me a new minivan with the insurance reimbursement. So even if I could drive, I had no vehicle until he followed through on his promise.

"Chris, are you going to drive me to the hospital to see the babies today?"

"I'll drive you there, but I can only stay for a few minutes. I have to go to work. After work, my mom and I have to move stuff from the old apartment."

"I was hoping to stay at the hospital for a few hours."

"Why? It isn't like you can do anything there, and there are things you need to do at home."

"One of the nurses promised to let me do kangaroo care today with the babies if they are off the photo therapy lights. It is supposed to be really good for them."

"Call my mom, and maybe she can pick you up later. I'm too busy."

Kangaroo care involved stripping the babies down to their diapers and placing them on my bare skin. It has been medically proven that skin to skin contact improves a premature baby's respiration and heart rate. My many anxieties went away as I held each baby one at a time inside of my shirt. They sighed contentedly, and I relaxed into the chair. For the first time since they were born, I really felt like a mom. I almost forgot about the horror at home. But when Chris's mom Jeannie picked me up I cried the entire way back.

At around age 28, I'd been diagnosed with clinical depression. Prior to getting pregnant I took a daily, low dose of an anti-depressant. However, I'd had to ween myself off it later under my doctor's recommendation. Understandably, I was super worried that I was pre-disposed to postpartum depression, or "the baby blues." The emotional and physical responsibility seemed like enough to bring on an intense case.

It turned out my babies were the only thing keeping me going. The love I felt for them was the purest, most uncomplicated love I'd ever experienced. Holding babies, with their skin touching mine, was better than any anti-depressant on the market.

Sensitivity Girl was both empowered and grounded by her kids. The nurses were surprised at how calm I was about everything to do with the welfare of my babies. The alarms didn't bother me, and I never freaked out about the inevitable setbacks in their individual conditions. I can honestly say I never, ever doubted that they were going to be okay. When I was with my babies I was as strong as a mother Ox. Able to ignore loud noises for hours and survive in a land of medical uncertainty. My sensitivity told me they were going to make it through this.

Sadly, the feelings of strength and happiness I absorbed from them tended to stay within the walls of the hospital. The kids were giving me power, but there was a force at home that seemed hell bent on doing the opposite. There was someone who had direct access to my heart, and he seemed to be doing his best to tear it apart.

The evening after my first dose of kangaroo care, Chris arrived home from work and immediately launched into a new verbal attack. He didn't understand why I wanted to go to the hospital for such long periods of time.

"We need to move the last of our things out of the old apartment, and I need your help. Most of it is your crap anyway."

"But Chris, the apartment is up a huge flight of stairs and I'm only allowed to do one flight a day. I'm not supposed to lift anything for weeks."

"Well, I just don't have time. If you want that stuff out of there, you are going to have to help. If not, we will just have to leave it all behind. Oh, and did you find out about that glass yet, or do I have to call the police?"

Oh my god, this was insanity! We had been living in an apartment at the school where I taught. We couldn't just leave a whole bunch of stuff behind, and I certainly couldn't call and complain about a stupid piece of glass!

The next day his mother drove me to the hospital, and I was able to kangaroo with all the babies again. This time was therapeutic for me to feel warmth and love inside. But visits there provided a stark contrast to my home life.

Every toilet stall at the hospital had a sign that haunted me each time I visited the bathroom. An eight and half by eleven sized sheet of colored copier paper read: *Are you being abused? Are you being called names? Are you criticized, or humiliated? Are you afraid of your partner? Are you being hit or physically abused? Are you being controlled or threatened?*

It was really hard to accept that I was in an abusive relationship, even though these posters described what was happening to me at home. I also knew I couldn't call the number. I didn't feel like verbal abuse was enough of a reason to ask for help, and my situation was so extreme with three little babies. My heart cracked a little each time I read it.

After the visit to the hospital, Chris's mom drove me to the old apartment. She had been working all day moving things out, but there was still a lot of stuff to organize and move. I set up a station in the kitchen and wrapped glasses and dishes in newspaper and tried not to fall apart. I was exhausted and still in pain, but I had to be strong and get through it, because I didn't know what else to do. By doing way more than the doctor wanted me to do and resting a little in between, we were able to move the rest of the items out of the old apartment before the August deadline. I naively hoped that things would finally improve after the move was completed.

Jeanine even joked about how stubborn I was, ignoring doctor's orders and working on the old apartment. I just smiled weakly. I couldn't tell her I had absolutely no choice.

The good news was the babies were growing stronger and healthier every day. The nurses at the NICU were amazing, and I spent hours at the hospital learning how to care for my children. I learned to change diapers, take temperatures, give baths, breastfeed, feed with a bottle, and even administer medicine. I tried to hide my anxiety about my marriage and constantly made excuses for the babies' absent father. It was true he was working long hours, but there were plenty of times he was just asleep on the couch at home. He seemed to be separating himself from all of us, and eventually, it was easier for me to just let him. The abuse had only been going on for a few short weeks, but each day I was dying a little more inside.

It is amazing how you can be abused by someone who treated you so sweetly, hit by someone who doesn't touch you, or abandoned by someone who is living in your home. It's even more amazing how hard it is to accept. Even now, years later, I find it difficult to type the word *abuse*. This abuse was coming from the man who actually sent me flowers after the first time we made love. Where was the sweet caring person for whom I fell so deeply?

What made it extra awful was that he knew me very well, and he found ways of forcing me to choose, or attempt to choose, between impossible tasks. He would push me to do things that might put my job in jeopardy, or even my principles. At the exact same time, he would push me to stay home and work on the house instead of going to the hospital to visit my tiny, sick babies. I remember these gut wrenching, emotional exchanges which left me feeling completely helpless and completely alone.

Each week Chris and I were scheduled to meet with a case worker and our children's doctors and nurses to discuss their progress. It was a very important meeting both of us were expected to attend. The morning of the first meeting, literally minutes before we had to get going, Chris announced I was not permitted to leave the house. He said a thunderstorm was coming and because our dog sometimes got upset during thunderstorms and could damage something in the house, I had to stay home.

"Chris, I can't do that! If Buddy breaks or damages anything I'll fix it. We need to go to this meeting!"

"Well, you'll just have to tie him up in the backyard."

"No way. It is supposed to get into the 90's today! We can't leave him outside!!"

"Too bad. You'll have to make a choice and make it soon. I have to be at work."

I started crying so hard I began to hyperventilate, and I fell to the floor. Finally, after what seemed like an eternity Chris said, "Fine, I'll take you to the meeting but if he damages anything you are never leaving him alone again. No matter what kind of stupid appointment you have."

We made it to the meeting in time, but I must have looked like a total mess and I felt like I had been in a car accident on the way.

I tried to be as strong as possible because I didn't know what else to do. It's true, at the hospital I had finally tapped into Sensitivity Girl, but outside of those walls I was helpless. I lashed out a few times because I didn't feel like I could talk to anyone about my concerns and emotions. I engaged in a coping mechanism I'm not proud of: I yelled at strangers.

For example, one day Chris was especially horrible to me in the morning. Later, as I walked up to the entrance of the hospital, I saw directly under the "No Smoking. Babies' first breath zone" sign a middle-aged woman puffing away on a Marlboro. I had to let her have it.

"Excuse me," I said.

She looked around, confused. I walked right up to her face, so she wouldn't think I was talking to anyone else.

"You are NOT supposed to smoke here. People bring little babies through these doors and THAT is why there is a sign."

I pointed to the huge display of words above her head.

"I was going to my car," she expressed with total surprise.

"It doesn't matter," I yelled at the back of her head as she scurried to the parking lot. "Babies don't need to inhale your smoke and neither do I!"

The employees at Babies R Us also felt the sting of my anger multiple times. I think I screamed at every single person who worked there at least once. There was one short little assistant manager I am fairly certain will run me over with her car if she ever sees me in public. Thank goodness there is such a high rate of turnover in the retail business, or I never would have been permitted to shop there again.

I just had so much to be upset and frustrated about. I was growing tired of asking Chris's mother and my parents for rides to and from the hospital. It was finally time for me to be able to drive again. The only bump was I still needed a vehicle, and Chris had the insurance pay off money in his personal checking account.

"You don't need a car right now. My mom can drive you to the hospital. The babies aren't going to come home for at least a few more weeks."

"But Chris, I feel horrible asking her for rides when

she lives 45 minutes away, and I am okay to drive."

"Well, maybe if you can get my piece of glass back for the end table then I will get you a van. Why haven't you called about that?"

"I'm not calling about the glass. You know I can't."

"You are worthless, you know that," he yelled. "What kind of mom are you going to be if you can't even do the simplest things right? No glass, no van. I guess it is just too bad." And he walked out of the house.

I sunk down on the floor and cried huge, racking sobs. I didn't feel like I could talk to anyone in my family about it because I was ashamed for him and his behavior. I didn't want them to ever know he could act this way. I figured maybe I could say something to his mother, at least she would give him the benefit of the doubt.

When she was driving me to the hospital a little while later, I tentatively brought up the subject. I only talked about the glass and the van and didn't really go into how truly awful he was being. She agreed that he was acting strange. She kept saying, "This behavior is not my son." She chalked it up to stress about the babies and work and all of this new, huge responsibility. I agreed, but inside I worried it was something more.

Later I decided that maybe I should talk to his cousin. She was as close as a sister to him, and she was good at cutting through bullshit and seeing things for what they really were. I called her on the phone and left a message. It felt like an eternity until the next day when she called me back.

She asked how the babies and I were doing, and I gave her an update. Then I gingerly posed the question, "Um, do you think that men can suffer from postpartum depression?"

"Why do you ask?" she said.

"Well, Chris is really acting peculiar," and I went into a full description of the past few weeks.

She sighed and said, "I can't believe that I'm going to ask you this, but do you think that maybe Chris is doing drugs?"

I paused a moment and answered her:

"It is totally possible. I haven't seen any physical evidence, but his behavior is completely out of control. He is verbally abusive, and it scares me a little. I have noticed that there is money missing from the bank account that really can't be accounted for. How do I find proof, and what am I supposed to look for?"

She gave me some advice on some things that could be signs of drug use, and suggested I search his truck while he was asleep.

I told her I would try, and then I posed the tougher

question, "So, if I find evidence then what do we do? I mean, something has to be done. I can't bring my babies home to a house where my husband treats me this way. I can't let the boys or Gabby think this is acceptable behavior in any way shape or form. At the same time, I need Chris. I can't do this on my own."

She explained that she had thought of all of this even before I called. Even over the phone in Florida, she had noticed Chris acting strangely. She suspected drug use and had even looked into some treatment programs just in case. Also, she was just as aware as I was of how stubborn Chris could be. Even if we had proof, getting him to admit a problem, and even harder, having him agree to get help, seemed impossible. The biggest issue was, even if by some miracle we were able to convince him to get treatment, I needed his income because of the triplets and the new house. My head was swimming.

She and I talked some more and even though we didn't come up with any solutions, it did feel good just to talk about it. I took her advice and looked for evidence of drug use, but I didn't find anything. The search was halfhearted because I knew there was little I could do even if I did find proof.

Meanwhile, the babies were getting better and better every single day. Chris was visiting them less and less, but I was at the point where I didn't have the energy to care what he did. Within two days of each other the boys were cleared to leave the hospital, and I was busy getting things ready for the big homecoming. Finally, with a little help from his mother I was able to obtain a used minivan, and I finally had the freedom to drive myself to the hospital. It felt really good to start getting my independence back.

Surprisingly, Chris went with me to pick up the boys from the hospital, but both times he left for work immediately after we brought them home. Their first week home was pretty crazy because they ate every 3 hours and it took them each a half an hour or more to finish a bottle, so really, every two hours I was feeding babies. Gabrielle was still at the hospital, and each day I would leave for at least two hours to be with her. Chris only ever helped if I begged or if one of the babies was really screaming. Most of the time he was either at work or down in the family room on the couch watching TV.

I was pretty exhausted and for almost a month I never got more than three or four hours of sleep in a row. Chris's mom helped with the boys, so I could go to the hospital, but she seemed to have very little sympathy for my lack of sleep. When I would request an hour or two to nap because I hadn't slept in days, she would say,

"Whatever. I only ever sleep for four hours or less, so I can't relate." It is almost impossible to nap when the person who is helping you in the other room seems to think you're being lazy. Chris was also letting her think he was helping me much more than he actually was. She seemed to believe his fictional version of our childcare situation, so she was unsympathetic to my cause.

There were moments when I would see the old Chris, but they were fleeting. If someone was visiting, he would treat me a little better. When he did help with the boys he was actually very sweet and funny with them, while I continued to suffer the backlash of his frustrations. Every once in a while, he would seem to want to spend time with me, and I tried to be very open to those times even though inside I was still upset with him. One evening he told me that the sous chef from the restaurant was coming over to meet the boys, and we could maybe all have dinner together and watch some TV in the family room. I jumped on the invitation because at least it meant he would probably be nice to me for a few hours.

We picked up Chinese food, and his friend from the restaurant showed up. She seemed nice enough. From what he had told me previously I knew that she had lived a pretty rough life. She was in an abusive relationship and had other problems. At least that's what Chris said. The boys were pretty good about hanging out while we ate and watched TV. Eventually it was their bedtime, and they were starting to get a little fussy. I told Chris and the girl that I was going to go upstairs, get them ready for bed and I would turn in before the midnight feeding in a few hours. I fed and changed the boys and got them settled. I took care of some little chores in the kitchen. Buddy, our border collie mix was sniffing at the door, so I let him out back to do his business. A few minutes later I walked outside to let him back in. What I saw while I was out there changed everything.

Chapter 17

I went inside and immediately confronted him. "Chris, I uh, I need to show you something upstairs."

He looked surprised and followed me up the steps. His friend was sitting on the couch watching TV. I took him into the bedroom, and I sat down on the bed and took a deep breath.

"Are you smoking crack?" I asked, but it really was more of a statement. His eyes widened, and he looked shocked.

"No! Hell no!" he said loudly.

"I let the dog outside a few minutes ago, and I could clearly see into the downstairs bathroom. I'm not stupid, Chris. I saw what you were doing, plain as day."

"No, well, okay. Yeah, I was smoking. But it was pot, it wasn't crack."

"Chris, I know what pot looks like and that was not what you were doing."

"Well, that is what it was."

"Okay, show it to me," I said calmly.

He looked panicked, but he agreed.

I followed him downstairs, and he started scurrying around the basement rifling through bags and boxes frantically.

"I can't find it," he finally said.

"Chris, it was ten minutes ago. You could not have possibly misplaced it in that short amount of time. I am going to sit here on this step until you show me what you were doing."

He turned to the girl, who was sitting very quietly on our couch, and threw up his hands. "She thinks I'm smoking crack."

I had asked him to see me upstairs earlier because I didn't want to make a scene in front of a guest. He had been alone in the bathroom, so I wasn't sure if this chick knew what he had been doing, but now I didn't care. She didn't say a word. I think she was smart enough to know there was nothing that she could possibly say in this situation. She may even have sold him the stuff, but it didn't really matter. He rifled some more and came up with a tiny pot pipe and handed it to me. I shook my head and gave him an annoyed look.

"Chris, it was dark outside, and the light was on. You might as well have been on a high definition TV. You were smoking something out of a long skinny glass tube, not this thing. I know what you were doing and by showing me this, it proves it. With your babies, upstairs! What the hell is wrong with you?"

He looked frantic but said nothing. I'd had enough so I turned to stomp up the stairs. "You can believe anything you want to," he called after me. "But I wasn't doing that!"

I peeked in on the boys who were quietly sleeping. I sank down on my bed and stared at the ceiling. It was made of plaster and finished in a rough texture. I could usually find some comfort in its abstract shapes and patterns. But now my heart was beating like mad and I had to absorb the events of the past hour. Believe it or not, I was actually a little relieved. It explained a lot about the past month: Chris's behavior, the missing money, his distance from his family.

It was also a relief to have some undeniable proof. Earlier, while I was standing outside watching him through the window, it was so clear what he was doing. In almost any other type of scenario he would have been able to explain himself and invent a cover story, but the events of that evening were crystal clear.

But my relief was also mixed with overwhelming sadness. My husband, the father of my three babies, was a crack head. How the hell did I get myself in this situation? Eastern European night trains and major surgery—even the mental health ward somehow paled in comparison to the fear and pain that I suddenly felt. I didn't cry that night because it was almost more than I could handle. I was furious with this man I thought I loved. Months later I might be able to understand how addiction can pull someone in, change them, and render them almost powerless, but in the moment, I could only feel disgust and shame for Chris.

The next day I had to drive him to the garage to pick up his truck as it was being serviced. He was trapped in the van with me, and he had to listen to me again.

"Just so you understand, I was only about two feet from you last night when you were in the basement bathroom. I stood and watched you the entire time you were in there, and what I saw cannot be denied. Just let me know when you are ready to talk about it."

He stared out the window with a conflicted look on his face.

"I suppose that explains where half of the insurance settlement from the Mitsubishi went," I said.

He tried to deny my statement and quickly explained that the money went into the purchase of his truck.

"Just stop it, Chris. I know that money came from your mother, and you bought the truck before the insurance check even arrived."

He huffed and looked back out the window.

"I thought I wouldn't have to talk about it until I was ready," he said. "I'm going to divorce you, you know! I'll leave you, and then where will you be?"

"Go ahead! That will make you happy, won't it? You won't have to worry about your family at all and you will have all of the time in world to be alone with your drugs! We will be better off without you!"

He looked shocked at my statement and fought back with anything he could think of. As we pulled in to the dealership he said, "You're just going to be a two-time loser! Two divorces!"

"I may be a lot of things, but at least I'm not a crack head."

He hopped out of the van and slammed the door. I knew he didn't mean a single thing he had said, but on the other hand I didn't really care. The current situation had to change.

Two hours later my cell phone rang. It was Chris, and I ignored it. Later, I wasn't completely surprised by his message: "I just wanted to let you know that whatever you saw, or uh, thought that you saw, well, it won't ever happen again. I'm going to try to come home early tonight, and maybe we can go and visit Gabby at the hospital." I wasn't unhappy to hear this message, but I didn't put much faith into it either. I knew it wouldn't be so easy for him to just "never do it again." I also didn't return the call. I wanted him to wonder if I had gotten the message or not. I needed some peace after the past few weeks, and at least I knew the balance of power had shifted in my favor. It sounds cold, but his actions had broken me a little inside, and cold was an easier way to feel.

His behavior towards me and the babies changed dramatically after that day. He was much more helpful and more attentive. He wasn't as irritable or negative, and he was mostly back to the Chris I had known before. I called his cousin and told her what I had discovered, and she was not surprised. I also told her I didn't really want to do anything about it at that time. I was exhausted in every way possible, and even though I couldn't exactly forget about the past few weeks or what I had seen in the bathroom, I just wanted to enjoy the fact that things were better. I really didn't care how or why.

Chapter 18

By October 2007, Gabby was finally home from the hospital. It seemed like maybe things were going to be alright.

"Chris, I need you!" I called to the family room. "It's important!"

My voice shook as I nervously wiped Gabby's bleeding finger. Chris ran up the stairs, and I showed him what I had done.

Gabby had been in the hospital for so long they had placed a semi-permanent identification bracelet on her little arm. I couldn't pull off the metal clasp, so I grabbed the scissors out of the kitchen drawer and figured I would simply snip it free. But as I snipped, she moved, and I also cut off the tip of her middle finger. At first, I thought I was imagining it, and then the blood started to flow. It was bright red and would not stop. My stomach lurched, and I felt dizzy.

My daughter has been home less than 24 hours, and I've already cut off the tip of her finger. I am the worst mother on the planet.

Chris grabbed a cloth and held it on her bleeding digit. She wasn't even crying, but I still wanted to throw up. I don't know if after weeks of acid reflux, IV's, and needles in the NICU the pain in her finger didn't register or if the cut was barely anything. But she didn't even seem to notice.

"Call the pediatrician," he said, "and find out what they want us to do. I will hold pressure on it and see if I can get it to stop bleeding."

I called the doctor's office and talked to the nurse on call. "Do not go to the Emergency Room. The doctors will not be able to put stitches on a cut that small. Just hold pressure on it with some ice, and call back if it doesn't stop. Don't panic. I get a lot of calls from parents who accidentally snip their children."

For two hours, Chris held her little hand and kept pressure on the cut. She cried a little only because she wanted to go to sleep and Chris wouldn't let her. He kept sending me out of the room every time I looked nervous and green. He didn't want me passing out because he didn't want another problem on his hands. Eventually the bleeding stopped, and she was back to normal. Chris handled the situation really well, and I was happy to have him there.

The day before the finger incident we'd brought Gabby home and got her settled into a routine. The doctors had recently discovered Gabrielle was suffering from acid reflux, and the condition had been causing her to set off low heart rate alarms at the NICU. They prescribed medication and we ordered a home monitor, so we could have the entire family at home. Chris went with me to learn about the monitor. He'd been showing more interest in the children and in me. I was still very angry and hurt, but slowly I was letting him win me back. I was anxious for life to settle down and for my family to be together.

Meanwhile, Gabby's reflux caused her periods of pain, but I was learning some tricks to make her happy. During the day Chris's mom would come and help with the babies, but at night I was pretty much on my own. My sister Linda would come and help on Thursday evenings, and I looked forward to that time.

My sister has a real talent for observational humor. She can tell me a story about her job, or describe something that was happening right in front of us with sarcasm and a deadpan delivery that can get me laughing until I practically cry. She visited me quite a bit when I was pregnant, and I used to worry she would make me laugh so hard I would go into labor.

Linda also has an amazing, caring side. Especially when it comes to children. She is not only a natural athlete, she is naturally wonderful with babies and children. She is another one of my super heroes. She was never able to have children of her own, and while this has been incredibly painful for her, she has used her maternal energy to care for others, and also to become a dedicated pet owner. I have yet to see her turn away an animal or a person who needs her. I've learned so much about how to properly mother my children from her. I learned from Linda that one does not have to give birth to children to love and raise them.

Chris was still working crazy hours and tended to mostly sleep when he was home, so the nighttime remained a series of catnaps and feedings for me. Unfortunately, I developed a clogged milk duct. I was given antibiotics and prescribed some rest. My sister offered to spend the night so I could get a little sleep. Even so, I got up with every feeding to help her. I couldn't in good conscience let her do that by herself.

The amount of work involved with the babies at night was a shock to my sister. As was how little Chris was helping. I was still in a place where I wanted to protect Chris, so I tried to sound blasé about the entire situation.

"Oh, it isn't a big deal. I rest when I can. It isn't that bad!"

Inside I was thrilled that someone was finally noticing how hard I was working and how little support I had from my husband. I was insecure about the entire situation, so it was nice to feel supported or at the very least understood.

Chapter 19

Fall 1995, I was alone in my loft apartment in Lancaster trying to rest after intense weeks of student teaching. The ring of the telephone interrupted my attempt at sleep.

"LuAnn, this is Niki. Did you read the newspaper today?"

Why do people ask me this question? I never read the newspaper.

"No."

"Bethany was listed in the obituaries. It said her death was ruled a suicide, by hanging!"

I slumped back on the bed. Bethany was my good friend and former roommate from New York.

Complete strangers at first, Bethany and I fiercely bonded after one phone call. We were randomly paired as roommates in the years before high tech college roommate connection programs and Skype. I simply called her up a month before classes started to talk about things like who would bring the VCR and pasta strainer. It turned in to over an hour of talking about favorite bands, boyfriend problems, and mutual appreciation of absurdity and sarcasm. I also could tell, right away, that

Bethany, like my other sidekicks, had sensitivity and possibly a bit of damage. I welcomed her into my posse with open arms.

Yet, she didn't hide out in black like me, and she didn't tend toward the dark side of things. She wore creative combinations of clothing: flowing skirts with Doc Martins and sparkly headbands, or flannel shirts with long underwear and miniskirts. But she had something more than a unique, unapologetic style—she was also overwhelmingly positive. Bethany saw the silliness and the good in everything. Whether making pasta, going to the store, or shaving your legs, it was all just more fun with her around.

Bethany taught me about embracing life and not caring what people thought. I had spent so much time hiding in dark outfits and looking down at my clunky shoes that I had missed the fact that life can be colorful, that there are always opportunities to smile. Bethany gave that to me. It was hard to fully grasp, to fully believe that this energetic bundle of life could have taken her own.

Six months before Bethany died, I'd lost another one of my sensitive sidekicks.

I had known Josh for about six years. We worked together at a local restaurant. He never walked into a room; he spun into it, like a Tasmanian devil. Josh was larger than life and sort of a legend in our town. Not the good kind either. He was one of those guys who showed up at every party, already knew most of the police officers by name, occasionally went to school, and was not exactly the boy most parents wanted their kids hanging out with. He was raised by a single mom and didn't really have to follow the same rules most of us did. Josh was wild.

I quickly uncovered a different side of Josh. The sensitive, thoughtful side. The guy who wanted to do the right thing and cared deeply about others. The friend who watched out for me and would have literally given me the shirt off of his back without a second thought. In all the time we spent together, he never once tried to hook up with me, never tried to get me to do drugs or anything else that I shouldn't or didn't want to do.

I think he liked that a girl like me, from a traditional background, who went to school every day, got good grades, and was destined for college, saw him not as the rebel, but as the amazing person inside. To Josh, I was actually pretty normal. I'd never thought of myself as normal before. He also made me appreciate the more traditional aspects of my life: as long as I didn't totally screw up, I had a very good shot at a solid future. My family was hard for me to deal with emotionally because I was sensitive. At the same time my family was a good family. I had a safe home to go to every single night. I had parents who cared about me and what I did. Parents who were both able and willing to pay fully for college. Josh helped me see that for many, it isn't so simple or easy. I was actually pretty lucky.

More importantly, I sincerely trusted Josh in a way I didn't trust most people. If I had needed him, there was not a doubt in my mind he would have been there for me. Even though he had rightfully earned a pretty crazy reputation, I felt safe with Josh around. His sense of protecting others seemed stronger than his sense of self preservation. I should have seen that his total willingness to lay down his life for his friends may be good for them, but not necessary all that great for him.

By the mid-1990's Josh had struggled with a drug and alcohol problem for a long time, and he was finally working very hard at staying clean. He had a lot of demons, and he found it harder to fight them off when he was sober. In the past, I think he used drugs as a form of self-medication. Without the medicine, with a clean system, it was difficult to deal with the messages in his head.

He talked about suicide quite a bit, but he also could be really upbeat about things. It wasn't that his friends weren't concerned about the suicidal stuff, it was that he also presented as so strong. I don't think anyone wanted to believe that he would really do himself in. He was a cool guy with lots of friends, and more importantly, like Bethany, he was full of life.

He had been planning a huge backpacking trip to Europe and he was working out well at a new job. Although many of his friends still worried about him, we were also feeling like things were going to work out. I was back in my hometown attending a local University and living at my parents' house. Many mornings, when I would leave for class, I would pick him up and drop him at his new job. I saw him nearly every day and he seemed very much alive.

The morning of his death I drove to the house he shared with his roommates. I knocked on the door and no one answered. I figured he either had gotten a ride with his roommates or didn't have to work that day. I didn't think a thing about it.

I found out later that day he had shot himself the night before. His death was devastating. In a single moment, he was gone. I had always felt like Josh was looking out for me, but I missed the fact that he needed me to look out for him. I hadn't fully understood the importance of a support system in one's life. He was such a physically strong person that I missed how his lack of a strong foundation, his lack of family support left him incredibly vulnerable.

Bethany struggled with some demons of her own. She had grown up in a home with an alcoholic father and although he eventually sobered up, she talked a lot about the effect her home life had on her. Her parents had divorced when she was young, which also had a huge effect on her relationships, feelings of abandonment, and insecurities. Because of her father's history with alcohol, she avoided drinking and drugs as much as possible. But we never seemed to need those things to have a blast.

When she moved to Philadelphia and started art school she found a boyfriend. He was a film major and very good looking. He was also known as quite the pot head and like to experiment with harder drugs. She described him as cool but in ways that made him sound like a selfish prick to me. Even though I hadn't met him in person, my powers told me he was bad news. He encouraged Bethany to start smoking pot with him and it quickly became a strong influence in her life. Not only had he coerced her into doing drugs, he also attempted to control every aspect of her life. He showed no interest in her family and friends, and most of us had never actually met him. He also didn't want her spending too much time with anyone other than him. She eventually dropped out of college and no longer seemed focused on her acting or other interests. The addition of this guy to her life seemed to be derailing it.

The agonizing part of all of this was that I hadn't spoken to her for a few months prior to her death. I had been so wrapped up in graduating from college and doing well at my student teaching that I didn't take the time to call her. It was also hard for me because she was so into the "pot head" culture and I had no interest in any of it. I was going to be a certified teacher soon and I wanted to be as far from that lifestyle as possible. It was painful to hear about this boyfriend of hers because I knew he was so terribly bad for her. She had a good family, a strong support system, but this guy, in one way or another had systematically cut her off from it.

Losing Bethany and Josh taught me a painful lesson. Not all super heroes make it. Sometimes the demons, the voices, the bad guys, they win. For some of us, the damage would outweigh our strength. Not all of us would end up in the X-men version of a retirement home. I wouldn't stop collecting sensitive super friends, but I needed to be aware that there was no guarantee of a happy ending for any of us.

Chapter 20

"You could probably use some rest. Your mother and I will take care of the babies while you try to get a little more sleep."

Chris was being really sweet and understanding that morning. My parents were visiting and planning to stay for the afternoon to help out around the house. Gabby had been home from the hospital for about three weeks. We had her in the bed with us and Chris was holding her. He rubbed his finger from the top of her little head down to the tip of her nose.

"Look how happy that makes her," he whispered. "She just closes her eyes and smiles."

He looked at her with pure love in his eyes. Then he packed up her monitor and carried her out to the living room. We had just had a great talk about the babies and about what our plans were for when I went back to work. Chris's mom had been helping out quite a bit, but she seemed unhappy with the situation. Chris and I discussed some possible solutions, and he promised to try to work things out, so everyone was happy.

While I rested, Chris and my mother worked on organizing the kitchen. They were both big fans of order and liked to try to put things in places that were convenient and practical. My mother is a great listener and Chris liked to talk to her. He found many people in this world too distracted to listen well, and he always felt she paid close attention when he spoke.

A few hours later I emerged from the bedroom.

"Chris, you look tired," my mother said. "Why don't you lay down now and LuAnn, her dad and I will keep an eye on things."

Chris smiled and nodded. He walked downstairs to rest in front of the TV. A little while later we heard strange noises coming from the basement.

"Is that Chris?"

"It sounds like he's snoring," my mom answered with concern. "Why don't you go check on him? He seemed to be having trouble catching his breath earlier."

I walked downstairs and found him sitting up on our futon sofa with his eyes closed and his mouth open. The noise that he was making was like nothing I had ever heard before from him, or anyone else. I shook him, and his eyes remained closed.

"Chris, are you okay? Wake up."

I put my hands on his face and shook his head back and forth. His eyes slowly opened, and he looked at me.

"Chris, are you alright? I almost couldn't wake you

up and you are snoring out this insanely loud sound."

"I'm fine. I'm just really, really tired."

"Do you want me to take you to the doctor? You don't sound right."

"No, I just need to get some rest."

I sat down beside him on the futon and he put his head on my lap. Then he wrapped his arms around my waist and closed his eyes. We stayed like that for a little while. It was the first time in months he'd cuddled up to me in such a way.

"Why don't you at least come upstairs and sleep on the bed? Maybe you will be more comfortable."

"Will you lay down with me?" he asked quietly.

"Of course, I will, now come upstairs."

He followed me up the stairs and I asked my parents to watch the babies for a bit while we took a nap. I laid down beside Chris on the bed and closed my eyes. About every ten minutes I woke with a jerk at his snoring. It actually took me off guard each time. After a while I realized that I couldn't rest at all like that, and I told him that I was going to check on the babies. He gave a groggy nod and curled around a pillow. About an hour later he came out into the kitchen looking completely wiped out. He pulled some steaks out of the refrigerator.

"Oh Chris, you don't have to make us dinner," my

mother said. "You look and sound terrible. Get some rest!"

"But I promised your dad that I would grill steaks tonight."

"No, we will be fine. Please, please get some sleep."

"Chris, are you sure I can't take you to the doctor," I asked. "I've never heard you sound like that and it is really hard to wake you." He assured us once again he was just tired, and he'd be going back downstairs to rest some more.

Eventually my parents went home, and I tended to the babies. Around 8pm I went into the basement and checked on him. He was still snoring. This time it was even harder to wake him. I pulled hard on his arms and pinched his leg. His eyes finally opened.

"Chris, are you positive that you are okay?"

"I really just need a few hours of sleep. I don't have to work tomorrow so I can sleep in."

One of the babies started to cry upstairs and I left him to check in. I got them all ready for bed and one by one I gave them their bottles. Around 4am the babies woke up, and I fed and changed them. I hadn't seen Chris for hours, but that wasn't unusual. The babies woke up again around 7 and I started to get them ready for their morning routine. By the time I finished I was a bit annoyed. Chris had been sleeping for almost 12 hours and I had been up every three or so. *It must be nice,* I thought! When I was finished I stomped down the stairs to wake him up.

It was dark in the basement and the TV was turned off. Chris was in the exact same position I had last seen him. When I shook his leg, it felt funny. Stiff and cold. My heart started beating faster.

"Chris?"

I put my hand on his arm and it felt the same way. I looked at his face. His eyes were closed and there was a little tuft of foam on his lips. His skin looked gray. I put my hands on his face and shook it. Nothing happened. His skin felt strange. I suppose the best way to describe it is that when you see someone alive every day for five years, you know when they are not.

I ran upstairs and found my cell phone and dialed 911. When the operator answered I almost didn't know what to say.

"My husband isn't breathing!" I said in a trembling voice.

"Ma'am, do you know how to do CPR?"

Technically I did. I'd taken CPR classes and been certified many times. But at that moment, I suddenly had no idea what CPR even meant.

"Um, I don't know," I think I said. "He's really cold and not breathing. I don't know what to do. I think he might be dead."

The operator tried to give me some instructions. I tried moving him, and even tried chest compressions, but I was pretty sure it wasn't going to work. I just didn't have the strength or desire to admit he wasn't going to wake up.

It seemed like seconds later the EMTs and the police showed up at the front door. I let them in and stood at the top of the landing. Less than a minute after walking downstairs, the EMTs started carrying their equipment back out again.

"He's gone," I heard someone say to an officer.

The officer walked upstairs and asked to talk to me.

"Tell me about what happened here," he said, flipping open a note pad.

I sat down on a rocking chair, sighed, and looked at my hands. "Last night he went downstairs to sleep and when I went to wake him up this morning I found him like that."

"Do you have children?" he asked

"Triplets. They are three months old."

His eyes widened. "He didn't get up at all to help you with the kids? Did you find it strange when you didn't see him all night?"

The look in his eyes alone told me he didn't think it was normal for one of the parents of newborn triplets to be "missing" for the entire night. What he would soon learn is that our home life was not normal.

"Um, he wasn't the most, uh, hands on father."

"Did he have health problems?"

"He was going to a neurologist who couldn't come up with anything," I said, "but I caught him doing drugs in the house a few weeks ago."

Then I went into the story of catching him smoking crack weeks ago through the bathroom window.

"So, do you think that it could have been a drug overdose?" he asked.

"Can you overdose from crack?" I asked because I honestly had no idea.

"Oh yeah," he answered.

One of the babies started to cry in the bedroom.

"Is anyone coming to help you this morning?" he asked.

"My mother is coming around 9am."

"Go and take care of your kids. I will talk to your mother when she gets here."

Chapter 21

I went back into the nursery and picked up Anthony. I sat on the bed and tried to comfort him, but I was feeling really numb. The strangest thing was that it wasn't a completely new feeling. For months, I had been dealing with incredible conflict and pain, only to immediately change roles and mother my children. I already knew how to turn off my emotions and pain in order to do my job. I was able to stay in this desensitized mode until my mother showed up.

"Oh LuAnn, I am so sorry," she said, and I started to cry. Nothing felt real. The officer came back into the room to talk to us. He asked if I had contacted Chris's parents and I shook my head no. He highly suggested I do it as soon as possible. This was a phone call no one should ever have to make.

Chris and his father had a distant and strained relationship. It had been improving very slowly but things were still not "good" between them. I never completely understood why. They had been very close when Chris was young, and Chris said many positive things about him. He even told great stories about experiences they had shared together. The death of his father's best friend, Lou, a short time before seemed to have started healing things a bit between them, but still, they rarely spoke. I had told him before we even became pregnant that if we had children, they would have a relationship with their grandfather. He agreed with me and admitted Steve would make a wonderful grandpa.

Chris was an only child and I knew his parents would take this extremely hard. He and his mother were very close, and I knew she would be devastated. I was a bit sexist in my decision, but I had a feeling that it would be better to call Steve and break the news to him first. I dialed his number.

"It's LuAnn," I paused. "I found Chris downstairs this morning and I couldn't wake him up. He's gone, Steve."

His voice cracked on the other end of the line.

"The police think you and Jeanine should come over right away," I said quietly.

He told me they would and hung up.

The officer came back into the room and explained they were searching the basement for clues as to what had happened. "From what we can observe it seems like he may have been dead for a few hours. I want you to know there wasn't anything you could have done. I have called the coroner, and his deputy is on her way."

It was bright and sunny in the babies' room, and they were smiling and cooing. It seemed as if I was looking at everything from really far away. I felt totally empty inside. Like part of me was missing. While the past months had prepared me to deal with crisis and responsibility, nothing could have prepared me for this. The crisis was not only bigger, it was permanent. When I tried to think about anything outside of taking care of my children, concepts seemed empty, like the blank space between the edge of a cliff and the ground hundreds of feet away.

I had worked so hard to protect Chris in the previous weeks and months. I had kept all of his anger, his behavior, his drugs, to myself. In one morning, everything changed. Chris was gone, and it was all out there in the open. Suddenly police officers, EMT's, and anyone else who was in my house needed to be involved. There were literally strangers combing through his stuff. Taking care of my kids was the only normal thing I had anymore. The rest of my life was completely and totally upside down.

The officer returned to the nursery and gave us an update. They searched his truck and found nothing inside. No drugs in the basement either, just a prescription pill bottle for Oxycontin shoved up under the sofa. Inside was a single pill that looked to the officer like Methadone. I would find out later that Methadone is used to help people who are addicted to Oxycontin. Because there was only one pill in the bottle, the officer suspected it might be a suicide.

I didn't agree with this theory at all. Just because a pill bottle is almost empty does not mean that someone has taken all of the pills inside of it at one time. Also, nothing about the events of the previous day seemed to go along with suicide. He was tired and ill for the entire day and I feel that if he had taken a number of pills on purpose, that everything would have happened much differently. I suspect he could have overdosed on something, but I was certain it wasn't intentional. Or at least that is what I wanted to think. What I had to believe.

Chris's aunt arrived and immediately began helping with the babies. I could tell it helped her to have something specific to do. Chris's parents arrived soon after that and they also seemed to need the distraction. It seemed like they were also very much in shock. The officer told me he had explained to both my parents and Chris's parents how I had caught him smoking crack. He also talked to them about his suspicions of drug overdose. I was relieved he had fielded a very uncomfortable conversation for me.

The deputy coroner eventually arrived and did whatever it was she had to do. She came upstairs, talked to me, and was very kind. She even played with the babies a little. It seemed like this occurrence, this death of a young father with the babies upstairs, was a normal everyday thing. In fact, the EMT's and Police also had this calm, experienced air about them. As if when they went home from work and their spouse asked about their day, they would just tell them it as a regular Wednesday.

The coroner explained that Chris was being taken out through the garage and would then be driven to the basement of a retirement home in Lancaster. That was where the coroner did his autopsies. The image would haunt me for quite some time: Chris, alone and naked, in the basement of some retirement home. I had seen enough CSI and Doctor G Medical Examiner to be able to picture it pretty vividly.

The Pastor from my parent's church arrived and sat down in the living room to talk to us and pray. It was the first time I noticed I was still in my pajamas. The house was filled with fully dressed people, and there I sat in a t-shirt and yoga pants. Like a horrible dream where I am at work in just my bra and underwear.

Then the police officer came into the living room and told us he had called a local funeral director, who was on his way. Pastor David whispered to me that he was from "the good" local funeral home. I hadn't known there was a difference. I never really thought about things like that.

It had only been about three hours since I had found Chris dead in the basement, and now a wide variety of people in the death business were visiting me. To this day I am still not certain how they knew so quickly I was in need of such specific services. Apparently, there is a death protocol, and it moves with efficiency.

The funeral director was also very kind. Luckily, I did not have to make any decisions right then. He just left his card and made an appointment to visit me on the following day to "make arrangements." The card sat on my coffee table. It was almost impossible to comprehend that I was in possession of such an item.

Suddenly I just wanted to be alone. I asked if it was okay for me to go lay down, and everyone unanimously agreed to let me rest. I lay alone on the bed and stared at the ceiling. I didn't even cry, I was so in shock.

What was I going to do? How was this possible? How was I going to care for my babies? Could I afford to keep us in our home? Where would we go if I couldn't? Was Chris really gone? Was this a horrible dream? How could he do this to us? I tried to close my eyes, but it didn't help. How could I rest when my life was falling apart?

It also dawned on me that I wasn't married anymore. My first marriage had taken many grueling months to dissolve. It had been a long and difficult road with plenty opportunities to change direction or put a stop to the process. This time I had gone to bed married and woken up unmarried. I literally became a widow overnight with no warning. No time to think about what it would mean for me to be a single parent. Like waking up in a new career with zero training and without consciously quitting the first job. I couldn't wrap my spinning brain around it.

A little while later the door opened, and my friend Shane filled up the doorway. A close friend of ours from work had heard about Chris's death at school. The police had contacted the headmaster, who had passed the information on to the faculty. Shane had left my school a few years earlier to work at a Christian school nearby. A mutual friend called to let him know that Chris was gone.

Shane came in and put his arms around me, and we both started to cry. I was so relieved to see him. He had always been there for me through the good and bad times of the past eight years. Sadly, though, his presence made the events of the morning all the more real. I was starting to think maybe I hadn't dreamed it all, and at that moment I became more frightened.

I still needed time to understand what was going on, but the world was moving too fast. I felt like I had to run to keep up, and I just wanted to stop and catch my breath and clutch my sides. Life wasn't going to stop and wait for me, though, so I had no choice but to keep moving with it.

Later that day I checked my cell phone messages. The County Coroner had called to express his condolences and his message was very kind. Based on his initial findings, he was pretty certain Chris had died from an accidental drug overdose. He explained the toxicology tests would take a few weeks, and I requested to be contacted when the results were confirmed. He also explained he could do a full autopsy, but he felt strongly that the toxicology would give him the answers he needed.

Chris was a very private person and I knew he would not want a full autopsy. Once again, I had seen enough on TV to know what is involved in such a procedure and the idea of Chris being split open with a Y incision and his organs removed and weighed was more than I could have handled. Then I agreed to have him cremated. I wasn't sure about it, but it seemed like the way Chris would have wanted things.

Eventually I emerged from my bedroom to find the house filled with people. Family, friends, and even neighbors I barely knew were stopping by. I felt 100%, completely overwhelmed and I didn't know what to do with myself. The next day, everything suddenly and shockingly slowed down to a crawl. I can only remember bits and pieces. What I do know is that I felt very supported during all of this, but I also felt very raw and fragile.

A few days later, Shane stopped by again, and he was very upset. He had learned about a few teachers from my school engaging in negative gossip about my situation. They were talking about the results of the toxicology, which was not even back yet, and saying bad things about Chris and drugs. Shane was livid. He wanted to rush to the school and set the record straight. I was flattered by his wish to protect me and to protect Chris, but the reality was, and is, you cannot stop or change this type of behavior.

I also didn't have any energy left to get upset. Instead, I calmed him down and said, "Shane, their behavior is typical. You and I are both guilty of sharing gossip in these types of situations. I am not surprised they are doing this. No matter what we say or do, they will continue to act this way. I know who my friends are, and we know the truth. Just let it go."

Shane was surprised by my reaction and he quickly relaxed about it all. I didn't feel good about what he had told me, and honestly, I happy to be the "star" of local dirt. But I learned a long time ago people will always gossip. Even when the information is true, you need to be at peace with it and realize whatever you do in life is going to be open for speculation. It still stings a little, but it's inevitable. If the information is not true, then, well, you know the truth and that is all that matters. It is more often the inner stuff, the real feelings of people that can hurt me. Gossip on the other hand, it is like the junk food of conversation. If people want to fill up on junk food, I'm not going to be able to stop them. When I've indulged in gossip myself, I tend to regret it later.

Chapter 22

"These are the urns we have available. The price list is in the back of the catalog. The other book is of cremation caskets. I don't want to tell you what do, but if cost is an issue I would choose one of the basic models."

I looked at the shiny books clutched very weakly in my hands. Everyone in the room was staring at me and I just wanted to go into my bedroom and hide. The funeral director was a very nice man. He was heavyset and had a quiet, sweet disposition. I know he was "selling" me something but I never felt like he was trying to upsell. The whole time my mind was screaming, "*I'm 35 years old! I shouldn't be choosing my husband's urn and casket!*"

"Do I have to decide on this right now?" I asked quietly.

The director explained that I did not, in fact, have to decide at the moment.

I found one of the hardest things about making decisions about someone's funeral is the finality. You can't do it over and you don't have a lot of time. You get one chance to "plan" something so important and you just want it to be right. Chris's parents really did not want to make any of the decisions, so I felt like the onus was on me to do the correct thing. I knew in my heart Chris would know exactly what he wanted but of course I couldn't ask him. I just had to guess and hope I was right.

His parents are very private people and they indicated wanting a small funeral, perhaps just family. They didn't even want anything written in the Harrisburg papers from his home town. It made me sad. I felt like they were doing this not for Chris, but to shelter themselves. I quietly and calmly disagreed with them. I explained that anyone who wanted to say goodbye to Chris should have the chance. It wasn't fair to Chris or to them to rob others of the opportunity for closure.

It was funny, Chris often said he didn't want anyone to make a big fuss over him. He'd tell me no birthday parties or gifts or anything like that. But every year, on the day or two before his birthday, he would almost always quietly say, "Do you think maybe we could invite just a couple people over tomorrow night? No big deal." And I would always do my best to put something together. Despite his resistance he seemed to have a deep need to know people cared about him, and I think he secretly worried that they didn't.

My parents' pastor came to my house so we could plan the memorial service. I knew Chris would not want a viewing. That one simple fact I was confident about. For the rest, I was at a loss. The pastor asked a lot of personal questions about Chris. It was awkward at first but soon we were all telling funny stories about him and talking about what a great man he was: his sense of humor, his sweetness and kindness. We talked about the things he loved. Chris was passionate about cooking (and eating), and he loved to watch the Philadelphia Flyers and Fox News. The stories made me smile, but they also broke my heart. For the millionth time, I thought about the fact that his three children would never get to know him. They would hear about him but never *really* know him as a person.

We decided to hold the service at my parents' church. The funeral director explained that when a young person dies there are often a number of people present at the service, and he didn't feel like the funeral home could accommodate so many people. I agreed to it, but I wondered how many would actually come. I had no idea if anyone would take off time from work, or how many people knew about it, and I just hoped, for Chris's sake, that there would be a nice turn out. I think most of us, if we are honest, hope a lot of people come to our funerals. It is that last moment of "I was here, I mattered to people, and I effected people."

The director requested I collect a number of photos

to be shown in a slideshow at the service, and also some framed ones to be put on a display table. Pastor David requested a song that would have been meaningful to Chris to play at the end. I agreed to collect these things and hoped I would have the strength and the clarity to do it right. At times like this there are many chores you can delegate to others, but some things you just have to do yourself. I knew I had to be the one to choose these things, and the task seemed daunting. I worried I wouldn't do it right, and it scared me.

Looking back, I think part of the fear came from guilt. Guilt that I hadn't really done a damn thing when I saw him the bathroom. I hadn't even looked into drug treatment programs. While I know in my heart his death was not my fault, I wished I had at least tried to help him. Done something. Yes, he was an adult, but I was his wife. I could have, I should have done more. I honestly never thought it would end like it did, and now it was too late to change it.

I knew I would have a lifetime ahead of me to think about the things I should have done better. So, in my mind, this funeral was my last chance to do something for him. This would at least be one thing I wouldn't have to spend the rest of my life re-assessing. Regretting. I just wanted to get something right for Chris. At the same time, I was also struggling with the roller coaster of crap Chris had drug me through over the past weeks and months. No one knew about the verbal abuse I had been suffering, and everyone was expecting a shocked, grieving widow of a perfectly sweet man. I wasn't quite in that place.

The funeral planning meeting was overwhelming, but later I was able to sit alone and think about things more clearly. I sat with the catalogs of urns and caskets and paged past the dolphin shaped vessels, the containers adorned with golf clubs or trains. While the old Chris may have found it funny and ironic to spend eternity inside a dolphin, I wanted to find something that felt more appropriate. I finally found a gray, pewter urn Chris might have liked—if it is possible to "like" something like that.

I used to love autumn. The crisp weather, and warm fall colors always made me so happy. We were married in October, and it was a special time for us. During those fall days, while sitting on my porch trying to plan a funeral, it felt so different. The breezes no longer felt crisp, they felt cold. The colors no longer represented warmth, they represented slow decay. I was cold, sad, scared, and angry, and fall got pulled in to my emotional state.

I became even angrier, but no longer with the

weather. I became angry with myself. I was being selfish. My feelings didn't change the fact that Chris was gone. They also didn't change the fact that he deserved a proper send off. Yes, he had screwed up, he had treated me horribly, and he had left us, but those actions were not the sum total of his life. I couldn't let the past weeks and months, along with my own negative feelings, erase the fact that through most of his life Chris was a sweet, sensitive, amazing person. I had to suck it up and do the right thing.

I went back to my porch and wrote Chris a letter. I had a lifetime to process the recent Chris, Chris the stranger. Right now, I had to celebrate the good one, the Chris I had known in my heart. The one I fell in love with. My fellow super hero.

I worked on the letter at various times during the few days that led up to the service. I would write, take a break, read over what I had, write some more, and eventually, after a little editing, I was happy with the result. I didn't know if anyone else would understand it, but I had to accept that it was really for Chris first, me second, and everyone else third.

"Urg," my mom whispered to me, "Could he drive any slower?"

I smiled and nodded, but honestly, I hadn't noticed.

I wasn't exactly in a hurry. My uncle and my father chatted away in the front seat of my uncle's Subaru. The extra time and slow pace of the drive helped me feel less sad and pathetic somehow. I stared out the window as my mom squirmed impatiently in her seat. I had hoped for rain but it turned out to be a bright and sunny day. I was surprised the beautiful weather made me feel slightly better. Maybe this would turn out to be more of a celebration than a funeral.

We filed in to the church and met the team from the funeral home. They showed me the table of Chris's photos and I saw a TV playing the loop of slides I had given them. There were pictures of Chris as a child, and a young adult. Photos of us together, on trips we had taken and during parties we had thrown. And, of course, photos of his children. I looked down the aisle and saw the gray and pewter colored urn that held Chris's remains. I tuned out the early attendees and made the slow walk down the center of the church. A large, framed picture of Chris from our wedding was placed behind him.

I rested my hand on the dull, rough exterior of the container, and cried. It felt so strange. He was such a presence in my life for so long. Now, suddenly, Chris's nearly six-foot frame and complex inner life was reduced to a pile of ashes in a vessel that wouldn't even reach the height of a young child. A wave of pure sadness washed over me, and it was suddenly hard to breathe. Tears rolled down my cheeks as I pressed my lips to my fingers and touched his urn to say goodbye.

I wish I could say I gained closure at that time, but those gestures felt hollow. It didn't really feel like I was saying goodbye to Chris at all. I just wanted to see him. To touch him, to talk to him, to hold him. I knew at that point, while looking at the gray thing, that I would never, ever have the chance again.

I also didn't feel like I was really there. I felt empty and lost. I slowly turned and walked back up the aisle.

There was a small room off to the side of the sanctuary that was reserved for our families. Everyone kept telling me there might be a lot of people at the funeral. As much as I wanted to see those who had made the time to come, and as much as I knew I should talk to them, I also knew I just wasn't strong enough. I knew it would be hard enough for me to walk down the aisle again and sit through the service without having an emotional breakdown. I suddenly felt incredibly small and weak and just wished I could be invisible, once again, and mourn Chris in my own way. My sensitivity to this completely foreign experience was emotionally exhausting.

His family entered the room. I could tell his mother was in a lot of emotional pain. She wore dark glasses and looked like she was barely holding it together. Seeing her allowed me to put my feelings aside and try to imagine what she must have been going through. She had lost her only son and now she too was experiencing these excruciating images and events. I knew I wasn't the only one in pain, but this was the one person who was probably suffering the most. She and Chris's father had chosen to let me make all the decisions about the service. I prayed I'd done the right things.

It was time for us to walk to the front of the sanctuary and take our seats. We filed out of the room. My sister took my hand. I took a deep breath and willed myself to move forward. I almost stumbled when I saw how many people had come. The church I had grown up in was fuller than I had ever seen it! Seats, balconies, and benches all full. Some were even standing. We made our way to our pew. I slid in between my mother and my sister. Chris's family had moved into the front bench, but I was glad to be in the second row. I felt more protected somehow.

I had been attending the church since I was a baby. When I was very young, it represented a soft supportive place. I attended Sunday School most every week, sang in the children's choir, and attended Bible school and other events. However, when I was around 12 or 13, when my brother and my family were going through an incredibly difficult time, the church no longer felt like the warm, happy place I knew as a child. I spent those years angry at God and ashamed of my family. Simply by existing, the "happy," "normal," families at the church made me feel like an outsider. I not only questioned why God hated my family, but also why these families were permitted such an easy life. At around the age of 15, I simply stopped attending. While I always believed in God, I had mixed feelings about organized religion, and this church in particular. My emotional perception of that negative time was unfairly projected to this place.

Yet on the day of Chris's funeral, the church returned to its supportive mode. I felt comforted by it. It wasn't full of perfect little families now, but people grieving the same loss. So much was happening that was unfamiliar and downright wrong, it felt good to be in a familiar place. Sometimes survival is about holding on to the tiniest thing for strength.

My children weren't physically with me that day in the church. They were with me in my heart and in my mind. They had kept me together through so much in their short lives, even though they were clearly too small to know or understand how much strength they had given me. Those tiny people, those fat wiggling little beings, those three-month-old kids who couldn't even lift up their own heads, carried me through one of the hardest moments of my life.

After the reverend's sermon, my brother came to the pulpit. My brother had come so far from the once troubled boy of our childhood. He had grown into an intelligent, handsome, and strong man. He was one my super heroes who had made it. The demons hadn't taken him down, and he was there to support me and speak for Chris. He stood tall behind the lectern and gave the most wonderful tribute. The following is from a copy he later gave to me:

"Good Afternoon. Thank you all for coming. Thank you all who have supported our families and my little Sister, LuAnn. Today we are here to honor Chris. Some of you knew him very well. Some of you knew the people close to him very well. To me, he was a Brother-in-Law, and the Father of my nephews and niece. His wife LuAnn, is my little Sister – a title she has not been able to shake in 34 years. In our family, as a girl, the first time you brought a boy home to meet your Parents, was a warm up to the moment of when you meet "the Brother." I can proudly say, from the first day I met Chris, to the last time I saw him in person (which happened to be a day I was covered in sweat, wielding a chain-saw in their back yard), Chris exceeded my expectations for approval as a companion to my little Sister.

"My fondest memory of him was at my Father's 70th birthday party held in Perry County. Chris & I were an awesome team on two grills. We had a blast making food for an event to honor my Father. He indicated to my little Sister that he also had a great time. On holidays, he became involved with projects my children were doing, never excusing himself to go "watch the big game." Perhaps that's because the Flyers weren't playing. He was always genuine when I talked with him and gave his complete attention to whoever he was having conversations with.

"On July 22, my little Sister and Chris made me an Uncle, Uncle, & an Uncle. Let us remember on Wednesday, not only did triplets lose their father, but, a wife lost a husband, companion, & lover. A mother & father lost a son. A grandmother lost a grandson. A cousin lost a brother. An aunt & uncle lost a nephew. A nephew & niece lost an Uncle. Friends lost a friend. Patrons lost a chef. Thousands of students going through and graduated from the Elizabethtown School District lost a "Legend" of a person whom they heard many stories about while learning in Mrs. Billett's classroom. Not to mention the Philadelphia Flyers lost one H-E-Double hockey stick of a fan. Sorry Pastor Wolverton.

"Through this tragedy there has been triumph. Family & Friends have done wonderful selfless acts surrounding LuAnn, Anthony, Charlie, & Gabrielle. Giving them all much needed love and support. Going to prove that building strong relationships with friends and family one day, just might pay off as it has with our families. Both families involved appreciate the outpouring support from the community and friends already received in these times of grief and will appreciate the continuing support as time moves on, pain lessens, and children grow.

"Chris, as long as I am alive, I will make certain your children share the same burden, with me as their Uncle, which your wife, my little sister LuAnn, has had to endure through the years as her BIG BROTHER. We will miss you, and will never forget you, and thank you for giving us a part of you to grow with as we all grow in our lives and relationships."

Kevin was so captivating and comfortable in front of what must have easily been 300 or more people. His words made me laugh and cry, and I was so incredibly proud of him. My brother had grown so much in the past

20 or so years. He was a married father of two and one hell of a guy.

After he finished the minister invited others to walk forward and speak about Chris. Shane walked up and shared fond memories of Chris and talked about the type of person he was and what Chris's life had meant to him. He ended his talk with: "Because I knew you, I have been changed for good," from the Broadway musical Wicked. His words could not have been more appropriate or fitting.

The last to speak was Chef Mark, the first chef Chris had ever worked with, who had taken Chris under his wing and taught him so much about what being a good chef was. Chris had always looked up to Mark and I was so happy to see him up there. He spoke of how focused and hardworking Chris was a chef. He also spoke about how nervous Chris was about being father and how scared he was about the idea of having triplets. The most important part was when he talked about how Chris had explained that fatherhood was making sense to him, that he finally "got it," and he felt like he could do it right. I was so incredibly proud. Not only of these men who spoke, but that Chris had such great people speak about him.

Finally, pastor David from the church stepped up

on the dais with my letter in his hands. I'd given it to him earlier that day and asked him to read it. I had always been very impressed with David as a public speaker and a minister. I was confident that since I did not have the strength to read them myself, he would do my words justice. The church was silent as he began:

My Dearest Chris,

It is hard to comprehend what I am about to write to you. It is two weeks shy of our Fourth Wedding Anniversary and our three beautiful babies are asleep in the living room. For the past few days I have been hoping that this is all a horrible nightmare, but I know in my heart that it is not.

Twenty-two years ago, I was a shy, awkward girl on the Mount Joy Swim Team. You were this handsome, shy, talented swimmer from another town. You were focused and humble and swam every race as if it were effortless. I was in total awe of you. When you gave me my first real kiss at the annual team picnic it became the most significant, important moment of my life.

Five years ago, through your amazing grandmother, you came back into my life. You were still fairly shy but at the same time very honest and open. We spent every date talking for hours and you were, and still are, the sweetest, funniest person that I have ever met. At our 3rd date, when you spread out the blanket that we were sitting on some twenty years before I knew that I was totally in love with you.

Right away you made it very clear to me how important your family and memories were to you. You not only shared hundreds of stories, you also took me to see the important places and locations of your best memories. Your grandmother's house, the Serbian Church, your great grandfathers tree in the park, the stream where Uncle John took you to fish, Hershey Park, Lou's old garage, and the little shop where your family bought sarma and other authentic Serbian food. And even though it was painful to talk about at times, you shared every detail about your long and amazing swimming career.

You also shared your love of cooking and food with me. You would spend hours planning, preparing, and cooking meals for the two of us. Even after you became a chef you still found the time and energy to create elaborate meals at home. Even though you constantly begged for honest feedback it seemed to break your heart a little if even the tiniest thing were wrong with a dish.

Every night you came home from work and would tell me about everything that had happened that day. You were so proud if you had created a successful dish or if someone liked even the tiniest snack that you had made. It was very difficult for you if things had not gone 100% smoothly. You were constantly striving to make things better, and I have never seen someone work harder. Anyone who has ever eaten something that you had prepared should consider themselves honored to have sampled something that you most likely poured your entire heart into.

It is very hard for me to accept the fact that you will never get to cook for our children. What I can take comfort in, and what I do know is that in the short time that you had with them no one could have loved them, cared for them, dreamed for them, worried about them and wished for them more. You were able to describe every moment and detail of their birth and you were the proudest father who ever stood in that hospital. You wanted everyone possible to see them, meet them, and know that they were yours.

There is so much of you here really, that it is hard to believe that you aren't all here. I know that I have said that it breaks my heart to think that our children won't know you, but the truth is that I will do everything in my power to make certain that they do know you. They still have a father, it is you Chris and you will never be replaced. You may not be here in body, but your spirit is alive and I know in my heart that you are watching over us and always will be.

I now have to find comfort in the fact that you are in heaven with Baba, your great grandfather, Lou and everyone else that has passed that you love. You are and always will be the true love of my life, and when we are together again someday I promise not to cover the bed in pillows, or snore, or make you sleep with a raft. I will watch Fox news with you, cheer on the Flyers, pull up my pants when I lean over, and hold on to you and never let you go. I will miss you and love you for the rest of my life.

Your dearest wife and friend,
LuAnn

As pastor David finished the letter he explained that I had chosen a song to commemorate Chris' life. There was a pause, then Elton John's "Rocket Man" played through the church speakers.

Chris's family, my family, and I went back into the room we had occupied earlier. It was very quiet. A few people chatted softly about how nice the service was. How everyone had done such a good job and so on. I felt good about how things had gone, and I also felt relieved that it was all over. We waited patiently until most of the footsteps were gone and it seemed "safe" to leave the room. Once again, I was reminded of how many people had taken the time to come. I hoped that Chris was there in some form to see how many lives he had touched.

The funeral was, in many ways, harder to get

through than the day I found Chris dead in the family room. While the service was certainly about Chris, it is not a stretch to think much of the focus was on me, the widow. I had to plan the thing and then stand and be present for it with tons of eyes on me. Yet, I survived it, with my kids in my heart every moment of that day. I also I did a pretty good job with my choices for the service. It feels almost shameful to admit, but at the end of the day I felt stronger than I had in some time. I hadn't left Sensitivity Girl at the hospital; in fact, I was feeling her presence increasingly every day.

Chapter 23

As we drove home from the funeral I experienced a familiar feeling of standing on the edge of another huge change in my life. And again, I felt alone. *How the hell was I going to do this by myself?* As a private school teacher my salary is decent, but in no way large. I had already been struggling to keep up with the babies while Chris was alive. Chris didn't have any life insurance or retirement savings. The reality of my new situation started to sink in the minute the memorial service ended.

There were so many visitors that I can't even begin to remember everyone who stopped by. Some were family members, others were friends or friends of family members, neighbors who I had never met, and even strangers who just wanted to show their support. I was surprisingly cordial and relaxed with everyone. Many were probably shocked that I wasn't crying every moment or zoned out like a zombie. I did my share of crying, but I knew I needed to be strong, not only for my children, but for everyone I loved. That's the responsibility of Sensitivity Girl: protect the fragile emotions of the others from the pain I might cause.

As soon as the shock of the days following October

10th subsided, everyone in my family and in Chris's family seemed to snap into action. My father immediately started to organize and figure out my financial situation. My brother continued to landscape my yard and organize my basement and garage. Chris's mother, cousin, and aunt went to work on the triplets' room while my family worked on the kitchen. Everyone took turns helping with the babies.

Many times, during those early days after Chris passed I sat quietly on the couch of my living room holding a baby and watching the chaotic remodeling. It was overwhelming to say the least. During one especially insane evening I remember turning to someone and asking, "Is it normal when someone's husband dies for everyone to re-enact Extreme Makeover Home Addition on their house?"

For the first time in my life I owned my own home, but it felt far from being mine. The place was immaculate during that time, which was cool, but I couldn't find a damn thing. I spent so much time calling people just to find out where the cat food or laundry detergent was hiding. My brother liked to regularly clean out my refrigerator, and more than once he threw away produce and lunch-meat I had purchased only hours before he arrived. I appreciated everyone's efforts and I know it made them feel good, but at times it contributed to my personal feelings of helplessness.

One of the oddest but also most inspiring aspect of those dark days was the fact the babies had no clue what was going on. They continued to grow, and they seemed to love all the extra attention they were receiving. They were learning to smile and coo and of course they didn't know they were supposed to feel sad. I would smile and coo right back at them but inside my heart was breaking. A huge part of their family was missing, and I hoped like hell they couldn't feel it. It also made me sad as they were changing so quickly. Changing in ways that Chris would never see. His life had stopped but theirs just kept chugging forward.

Chapter 24

I seriously had no clue how to raise infants. Let alone three at one time. I was a youngest child, I had done some babysitting, but only with kids five or older. I never found babies all that interesting. I was more excited when a friend had a new puppy or kitten. Prior to my own children, I had never changed a diaper. On anything. Dogs just went outside to relieve themselves, and cats were practically born with the understanding of a litter box system.

Once my tiny tiny children were home I didn't exactly have time to analyze the situation or pop down to the library and study up for hours on end. I couldn't even think about how to carve out time to go to the monthly *Mother's of Multiples* meetings in our area. The only thing I had was the sheer determination to not fuck it all up. To not screw up my kids if I there was anything I could do about it.

Sensitivity is not the only super power in the world. I've known people who seemed to be born with the natural virtue of baby raising. Individuals who would hold infants as a career or Olympic sport if it existed. Experienced Superheroes who had the power to care for and nurture new life. I needed access to these skilled mentors who knew what they were doing and who were willing to share their secrets and expertise to an overwhelmed, nervous, single mom.

Chris's mother had originally planned on being our unofficial nanny. Yet with her son's death, and the sheer magnitude of the task, it seemed better to call in recruits. She was also a retired teacher and used to being in control. As weakened as I was from recent events, I knew it wasn't a good idea to have someone like that in my home all day every day. One, or both of us would not have survived. Also, whether she would have admitted it or not, she needed time to process and grieve over what had happened to her son.

I lived in, and came from, a small town. Word had gotten out quickly about my situation, and friends, family, church members, neighbors, and other great people were showing an interest in helping. What started out as a few helpers to fill in some holes in my babysitting schedule soon became a legion of qualified childcare volunteers. People had so many reasons for wanting to help. Some had grandchildren who lived far away. Some had lost spouses or loved ones. Others just really loved babies and couldn't wait to pitch in.

I had spent my life assembling a small team of

sidekicks. People who shared my sensitive nature and whose bond I used for strength. I had gotten along well with my little sensitivity squad of friends. In this situation however, it was no longer enough to rely on my closest friends. Practically overnight my support network grew from a small team to an entire army.

At first, I was anxious about the prospect of having a bunch of strangers in my house and never being alone. I had spent a significant part of my life laying low and taking care of myself. My sidekicks became a vital support system, but at the end of the day I often felt like the responsibility for me was on me. It worked okay. I was scrappy. I was a survivor. As I had during many points in my pregnancy and after the kids were born I reminded myself it wasn't just about me anymore. Scrappy probably wasn't quite enough. Sometimes, to do what was best for all of us, I had to be willing to go outside of my comfort zone, look beyond myself, and do what was best for my family.

Chapter 25

In November 2007 I went back to my job as a photography teacher at the boarding school. I was nervous at first. There had been a lot of administrative changes in the few short months I was gone, and I wasn't quite sure how they would affect me. I had gone through so many changes of my own since the previous spring when I needed to quit working and start my maternity leave. I was getting used to being home with the babies. Even with the troops back home taking care of my kids my life still felt wobbly.

School relieved some of my maternal pressures. I'd missed my students so much and it was uplifting to be back with them. I felt more like myself than I had in a long time. I was also more autonomous at work than at home. My students did not need the immediate, sometimes unpredictable care infants did. At work, I could eat lunch in a relaxed fashion with my co-workers and I didn't have to cook it myself. I had time to read and write emails and even listen to music.

Returning to work was the closest to "normal" I had been in months. Yet normal was a huge reminder of my life with a husband. My life before it completely changed.

I had few if any good memories of Chris and I at my house, but suddenly I was back in a place where things had once been good. This allowed a new layer of grief to take hold.

I sometimes found myself looking out the window of my classroom waiting to see Chris walk across the campus in his chef gear on his way to work. Often, prior to my pregnancy, he would stop by my classroom and chat with me right before he left. I missed him much more at the school than I did at home. Work was the only part of my life with Chris which hadn't changed dramatically.

Even with all of the support, including my father keeping an eye on my finances and bills, even with donations from people and churches, I often felt like I was living on the emotional edge of what I could handle. That is the problem with the ability to appear like everything is okay. I wanted everything to be okay, but much of the time it was an act.

I believed in the self-fulfilling prophecy. If I faked it long enough it would eventually become reality. People would see me from the outside and assume that I was completely stable and could handle anything. Sometimes I wasn't so stable, and I could have really used a shoulder to cry on, but I kept pushing through. It was more of a fake it til I make it or fake it until I implode. I was terrified of failing, but deep inside I felt close to defeat many times.

Parenthood, under any circumstances requires extreme balance. All of us, parents or not, work at balance in our lives, but during the tough times the space we balance upon can become quite small. The problem with teetering on that small space is how vulnerable it makes us to the possibility of getting shoved over. Sensitivity causes the shoves to feel stronger than they are, which leads to overcorrecting and makes it even harder not to fall. The other factor is what surface waits below us. Some days I felt surrounded by pillows of caring people, other days by shards of glass. It's possible to be around people all day long and still feel isolated.

Early spring 2008.

"I'm just so damn lonely," I told Shane. "I feel strange because most people really have no idea what I've gone through. Chris died only six months ago but I lost him long before that. I miss having someone hold me and kiss me."

So why didn't I just hook up with Shane? Why

didn't I simply walk off into the sunset with my best friend?

It's a reasonable question. Shane is handsome, smart, funny, and he loves my children. And don't think he didn't ask. More than once, right after Chris died, Shane offered to do the honorable thing. He wanted to marry the me and give my children a father, and their mother a husband. It was incredibly sweet and incredibly brave of him. But he was doing it for practical reasons, traditional reasons, and it wasn't the 1800's.

I've always known it was a straight forward friendship between Shane and me. One of the benefits of the power of sensitivity is the ability to be deeply in tune with my feelings. I had learned the hard way, in my first marriage to the pretty boy narcissist, that a marriage of convenience is not for me. Even through all the pain that romantic love had caused me, I still believed in it, still believed that I deserved it. And I missed it.

In that year after Chris died, the feeling of emptiness was overwhelming at times. In late February I created a halfhearted profile on a singles website. I didn't want to find a date that way, but I had no idea how else to go about it. I had very little free time so the ability to hang out and meet someone in a bar was virtually impossible. I also didn't want to meet a guy in his mid

30's or older who hung out in bars looking to pick up desperate women. I just didn't know what else to do.

So, I created the profile spontaneously and totally in a clueless and hurried style. I didn't bother to read the directions or the rules. I figured if some guy saw my profile and was interested, I would get an email message from the site. For weeks, I didn't even bother to log on. The whole situation felt desperate, and I was busy at work and at home.

One day I was feeling especially lonely and sad, so I decided to log on just to see who was out there. In the top corner of my profile page I noticed a link where I could view the men who had viewed me. I clicked on it and discovered that a couple of guys had "winked" at me in the previous weeks. I clicked on one of the men who looked interesting and read his profile.

Ken was a local artist in his early 40's. He was well-read and well-traveled, and seemed interesting. I winked back at him, but his profile indicated that he hadn't visited the site in a few weeks. I had no idea if he would even see my wink. It had been almost a month since his electronic gesture and I figured he must have assumed I wasn't interested. I logged off and wandered around the house finding chores to do and thinking about how I may have missed a chance to meet someone interesting.

The next day, there was no response from the guy. I figured I didn't have anything to lose at that point, so I decided to get inventive. I looked up his website through the dating profile and found his contact information. In the email I apologized for not knowing what I was doing with the whole online dating thing and hoped that he would want to correspond.

A few hours later I was happy to see a response in my inbox. In his message, he included many questions. Questions to which my answers would send most guys running away screaming. "How many kids do you have?" "How old are they?" etc... I contemplated how to answer. I hoped I would have a bit more time before I had to spill any potentially frightening info, but I was suddenly confronted with it, and I had to make a decision.

I decided plain old honesty was the best approach. I couldn't exactly hide the truth, so I figured, what the hell. I told him about my kids, the fact their father had died, that it was complicated, but I was not in the market for a new father for them. I just wanted to go on some dates with a nice guy. I crossed my fingers and hit send.

Everything I had been told about on-line dating, along with my past dating experience, warned me to take things slow. But when it came to dating mode, I only had the pre-mommy me to rely on. My old standby methods of spontaneity and impatience pushed me to send a message expressing my interest in seeing him face to face. Once again, he seemed really cool about it and agreed to meet me.

We made plans for a quick lunch at a local coffee shop and then possibly to meet up again later. I had seen photos of him on his website and he looked cute. Not that it really mattered. He was and artist and seemed cool, so looks were secondary. I am usually much more attracted to personality and brains than looks, and I already liked the little bit I knew.

I slowly opened the door and scanned the cafe. There were many older patrons, and some moms with their young children. Sitting by the wall was a cute guy with glasses, a mug of coffee, and a book. It had to be Ken. I smiled as he stood up, and I extended my hand.

"LuAnn?" he said with a smile.

We shook hands. It was totally awkward, of course. But not terrible. We ordered our food and sat down. We had a nice lunch and talked about some of the things we had mentioned in our emails. Travel stuff, life stuff, family stuff, etc... When it was time for me to return to work he walked me back down the street to my school and gave me a hug and a little kiss on the cheek. It felt nice.

The whole situation was nice and a bit exciting. I

felt young again. I was however, old enough and wise enough to realize this man was not going to turn into the love of my life. He smoked, drank in dive bars quite a bit, had a pretty erratic schedule, and seemed a bit unfocused. Not exactly the perfect man for a single mom of three. On the other hand, he was cute and nice, and easy to be around. It was fun. Just what I was looking for at the time.

Ken and I went out a few more times, and it was nice. Sadly, because of that desperate need for affection and connection I smothered him with texts and emails and scared the hell out of him. He eventually gave me the brush off, which I totally deserved. I came on too strong and was carrying a boat load of baggage. In my mind I was a cute, adventurous photography teacher; he saw crazy eyes and desperation.

I was upset, because honestly, I had rarely been dumped before. I didn't quite know what to do about it or how to feel. But I got over it fast. I had already been through so much worse. I learned a lot about how I was truly feeling and about the fact that I wasn't as "good" as I thought I was.

Looking back on it now it's easy to see I was so not ready for dating at that point. I was just so damn lonely, and it was totally stupid of me. I saw Ken months later at the grocery store and ran the other way.

It continues to amaze me how often, in the year after Chris died, I convinced myself I was doing okay, when in reality I was an emotional mess. I didn't understand how I could be so completely sensitive and so completely dense at the same time. So much of my power came from feeling, from my heart, and not enough from my head.

Chapter 26

By the time the children were one and a half it was easier to take care of them. The evening help wasn't all that necessary, but it was still a valuable emotional support for me. After working all day, it would have been overwhelming and lonely to come home and take on the parenting of three. Instead, I had wonderful, positive adults to help me and talk to me. To this day people ask me how I did it, and they want to know how bad it was. Honestly, I had it better than most moms of little kids.

In addition to the assistance I was given, there was a skill I had that made life easier: managing tricky timing. Swimming is about time. Swim practices are all incredibly focused on the clock. Four 50's on 60 seconds, 12 x 100's on a minute 30, that kind of thing. In practice, I would always find myself doing the calculations in my head. "If my average 50 during practice is on 40 seconds, and I have 60 seconds per 50, I need to push it to get at least 20 seconds of rest between each." When a swimmer meets another swimmer the question of one's best time in an event is almost always part of the conversation.

My first job at 16 was at a hostess in a busy fine dining restaurant. Usually by the middle of the week the reservation lists for Friday and Saturday were booked solid. Even with the tables laid out in the reservation book, there would always be quick changes. Timing and fast thinking was everything. I was good at it, and I enjoyed it. So much so that I became head hostess at 17 years old. As I mentioned previously I had worked in restaurants for nearly all my working life, mostly as a hostess. I could have made more money as a waitress, but I was so good at reservation books that it always made more sense for me to do that job.

And then there's photography. Almost every aspect of any type of photography is about time. Film or digital, one still needs to think about shutter speeds, film speeds or ISO, and whether a shutter speed is low enough to require a tripod. Film photography is even more time-sensitive. Different types of film and photo paper require different developing times. When printing photos in a darkroom one does time tests for each photo, and timers are everywhere.

So how does timing impact motherhood? Well, I have become aware of how long it takes to do almost anything we do as a family. For example: if we were invited to dinner at 6pm in the next town, I could instantly calculate how much time it would take us to get ready to go, any incidental activities like feeding the cat, and how long it would take to drive to our destination.

Yes, kids are unpredictable. But I know my kids well. I know Gabby can do things like putting on shoes and brushing her teeth quickest, especially when the destination is exciting. She usually starts getting ready first and helps to model the act of preparation for the boys if they are paying attention. Charles needs guidance but can be consistent in the amount of time it takes him to do things. Anthony takes the longest to do things and often has questions, so I need to start working on him to get ready early while supervising Charles.

I learned that as a Mom, I could put my powers of sensitivity to practical use. I knew my kids well enough to anticipate their behavior. I combined that with my time calculation skills, added a few extra minutes for surprises, and most of the time we didn't run late for anything and lived with lower stress levels. I was not only seeing that I had the skills to be mom, but I was kind of good at it.

I had lived so much of my life based on my instincts and emotions. Motherhood allowed me to see that I had been developing other skills, other powers over the years. Going into my life with kids I had assumed I was completely unprepared, but I was wrong.

I was never a physically organized person. My bedroom, my desk had always been a mess. Yet my mind was organized. I wasn't just born with each super power, I developed a few along the way. I was cultivating the power of prediction. My strengths were expanding, and thank God, as there were still more battles for me to fight.

Chapter 27

2008. A handsome man was calling my name. My father and I stood up. I was grateful to leave the crowded waiting area at the Lancaster Social Security office and enter the maze of cubicles and workers reserved for people with appointments. Even though I had very legitimate reasons to be at the S.S. Office, I ended up feeling small and desperate. I felt as though I was asking for something that maybe I didn't deserve.

To be fair to Social Security, my situation was very confusing. When my children were born I received benefits because they were premature and low birth weight. When Chris died the children were also eligible for benefits because they were under the age of 18 and had a deceased parent. It was additionally confusing because they are triplets and only one digit separates their social security numbers. This perfect storm of facts and situations created quite a bit of confusion for a long time.

Some months we were paid too little, other months we were paid too much, and most of the time no one, including me, knew what was going on. Often, I would receive three letters stating that the children had been underpaid and would be receiving three additional checks.

Sounds great until a month later, when I would receive three letters explaining I had to pay the money back.

You might be saying to yourself, "It was their mistake. Why would you pay them back?" Well, when S.S. wants its money back they threaten to never send you another payment until the problem is resolved. So, if they wanted me to pay them back, I paid them back. Most of the time we were talking about hundreds of dollars, and early on I relied heavily on that money to pay my bills and put food on my table.

When Chris died I didn't know how I was going to keep us afloat. He usually brought in more money than I did. Luckily S.S. could provide amounts just a bit lower than what he would have brought home, and they did so tax free. Sadly, in his final months, when Chris cashed his paycheck I am assuming a significant amount of this money went to his drug habit. Without the added expense of crack cocaine and who knows what else, I found it possible to make ends meet.

I also had the added benefit of my father taking charge of my finances. There were many reasons this was important, even necessary. The first and most crucial reason was the fact that I was terrible at financial record keeping. With my schedule as a full time working mom with three kids to keep track of there was really no way I could keep track of my money and spending in a consistent way. One of the other reasons was the fact that my finances became very complicated after Chris died. Accurate records of spending for the children needed to be tracked, along with taxes, insurances, etc...

While I shy away from such things, and many people struggle with money matters, my father lived for finance. He kept track of almost every penny I spent. I handed all bills and receipts to him, and he pretty much knew about everything I spent money on. He was understanding about it all, at least at first. Unlike the old days with the cereal, he never made judgments or comments about what I bought. Occasionally, he would offer suggestions on how to save money, but they were only suggestions.

It went well this way for almost two years. My father kept things under control and kept me posted on potential problems. It was a little confusing because the guardian (or in my case parent) of the individuals receiving Social Security payments needed to use the money for things specific to the beneficiaries. One must also do their best to spend the money every month. So, there were several times my father had to tell me to be sure to spend the money. There was often a concern I wasn't spending enough.

I wasn't fully prepared for the day my father returned to the man I had known when I was a child. I came home from work and barely had my coat off when he laid in to me. In front of my kids.

"Your spending this month is out of control. Don't you have any idea how hard I'm working on this stuff? Don't you appreciate what I'm doing for you? What is wrong with you?"

His favorite expression, one he had used on me my entire life: "What is wrong with you?" That phrase was a shot directly to my soul. When my father would yell at me, at any age, it wasn't the volume or the words that would destroy me. My father could bore into me with a look that was deadly sharp and ice cold. The expression in his eyes would hold the deepest imaginable shame and contempt. It was a look that could convince me I was the most worthless, selfish, stupid person he had ever come across in his entire life.

I firmly asked him to leave house, finished unpacking my work bag, and started dinner for my kids. All the while, I was shaking. Not from shame, but from anger. I had spent two years cultivating a happy, supportive home for my kids. That afternoon, in front of them, he broke that bubble. And it was never going to happen again.

Later that evening, after the kids had gone to bed I sat down and wrote him an email. I poured out the pain of my childhood. I wrote about the verbal abuse and anger I had lived through as a child. I also let him know, definitively, that my children would never be raised in an environment like the one that had left me insecure and weak for such a large part of my life. It wasn't about me anymore, it was about them. Just because no one could protect me from the anger and negativity didn't mean I wouldn't do everything in my power to protect my own children. I wrote that if he ever spoke to me or any of my children like that again, he would never see them again. If he chose not to help with the finances anymore, I would figure it out on my own, even if it risked sending us to the poor house. And I meant every single word.

It took a few days for my father to process this. My mother had to explain the email to him, to translate what he read into concepts he could understand. He never knew how hard he was on me, the negative impact of his treatment of me, or how much of my life I had spent healing and learning that I was better than he had lead me to believe. It is possible he simply believed I was being too sensitive. Growing up, when I expressed emotions and feelings, he would become irritated. Tears really seemed to make him angry. I wasn't sure, even after the email and my mother's assistance, that he would ever understand.

Whether he got it or not, it didn't diminish the importance of my words. I am most sensitive to the emotions and behavior of those with authority over me. Whether it be professional authority, or a form of relational authority. I developed this vulnerability after years of feeling bullied by my father. This reaction to authority has been one of the most difficult obstacles of sensitivity. Standing up to him, to the most significant of negative authority figures, was a huge step toward pushing past the negative. After that day, it felt like there was no dragon I could not slay.

Chapter 28

Naps. I love and always have loved naps. When you have young children, naps take on an even bigger, more glorious meaning in one's life. It was fall 2009 and my two-year olds were napping away the afternoon. The house was warm and quiet. Life had been humming along well for months, when suddenly there was a knock at the door.

People knocked on my door all the time. My house had developed over the years into one of those places where people just stop in randomly. I loved it that way.

I tiptoed down the steps and opened the door, expecting to find a friendly visitor. Instead it was the postman with a letter.

"Certified letter from the Diocese of Harrisburg for LuAnn Billett?"

"I'm LuAnn."

"Sign here please."

I got a little excited as he handed me a fat envelope. I don't think I'd ever received a certified letter before. Perhaps it contained some sort of check or award. I should have been paying better attention to the Diocese part, which indicated something Catholic. I am not

Catholic, and the Catholics certainly were not sending me an award.

I ripped the envelope open while walking up the stairs. My confusion gave way as I read the information enclosed. My first husband was looking for an annulment, so he could be re-married in the Catholic church. He wanted to pretend our marriage never happened, and he wanted to make it official. At first, I wasn't upset or even surprised. The guy lied as often as most people blink, so why not get a lie certified? This was soooo up his alley.

My first husband wasn't Catholic, so he must have fallen for someone who was. We divorced in 2002. Of course, he'd moved on and wanted to re-marry. Not hard to believe. I almost signed the ridiculous paper and threw it in the mail. Almost.

Later, when I had more time, I read the paperwork a little more carefully. It all seemed straightforward until I noticed a yellow page covered in my ex's distinctive hand-writing. It was a copy of his petition to the Diocese. On one line he'd had to state a claim regarding the invalid nature of the marriage between us. He'd written: "Intention against the good of children on the part of my wife."

MY WIFE! It was at that point I got pissed.

In the Catholic tradition, *intention against the good*

of children means withholding sex without contraception in order to prevent intercourse that could produce children. In other words, I was on birth control during our marriage and did not get pregnant. While that was in fact true, it does not tell the whole story...or even part of it.

Condition Against "the Good of Children"
(Canon 1101)

To enter a valid marriage, a person must place no conditions or limits on the essential elements of marriage, which includes a radical openness to children. This ground can be considered if one or both of the spouses placed a condition on childbearing, such as a limit on the number of children to be born in the marriage. The condition must be present from the beginning of the marriage, and measures must have been taken to ensure that the condition was, in fact, met.

Did either you or your former spouse express any condition or intention to limit the number of children in the marriage (for instance, "I will marry you on the condition that we have only one child")? Was this an absolute intention or condition, and not just a vague thought about the future? Was this a firm intention or condition, and not negotiable or changeable? Were there means taken during the marriage to guarantee the fulfillment of this condition or limit (such as contraceptives, sterilization, or abortion)? Was the condition actually fulfilled?

It became clear to me, that I had to challenge what my ex had written. I also felt I had to let the Diocese know what really happened, and why our marriage dissolved. It certainly wasn't because he wanted kids and I didn't. It was, in fact, a completely different paragraph found in the Canon.

Intention Against "*the Good of Fidelity*"
(Canon 1101)
A valid marriage includes three essential "goods"— children, fidelity and permanence. If one or both spouses entered marriage with the intention to exclude absolute fidelity, this ground can be considered. Fidelity or exclusivity in marriage means to have only one's intended spouse as a sexual partner for life. Absolute fidelity prohibits openness to any other sexual relationships. When one enters marriage with the intention of excluding such absolute fidelity, remaining open to the possibility or thinking that they may choose

whether to have other sexual partners, the marriage is invalid. It is important to note that what invalidates the marriage is the intention, present from the beginning, to permit infidelity – not actual infidelity. Adultery itself is not a ground of nullity.

Infidelity and deceit were grounds for annulment according to the Catholic church, and my ex had chosen not to mention that aspect at all on his little yellow paper. Trust me, I read it carefully. I checked.

I sat down and thought about what to do next. The envelope included a lot of information about the annulment process. It was clear that if I ignored the papers and did nothing, the annulment would proceed and most likely be granted. I also had the option to completely oppose the annulment, but I would have to cough up any fees that the church deemed necessary. Then there was the third choice: dispute the grounds of the annulment and give my side of the story but leave the final decision up to the Catholic Tribunal. I liked that one.

I composed a letter to accompany the paperwork I would return to the Diocese. In it, I explained why our marriage had dissolved and what the real grounds were for an annulment. I didn't even blame it on his potential infidelity. I blamed it on his lying. I also explained how his claim that our marriage failed because I would not give him children was proof he was still lying. I explained I was not opposed to the annulment at all; I just couldn't agree to the grounds that he was claiming. Basing his annulment on a lie would not be the best way to start his new marriage.

The process seemed so formal and was so unknown to me. I quickly started grilling all my Catholic friends about annulments. Surprisingly, no one seemed to know much about them. A few had relatives who'd gone through the process, and the consensus was that it was long and expensive. This information did not concern me. I wasn't getting married any time soon, and according to the information provided, the process wouldn't cost me a penny if I didn't outright contest it.

A week or so later I received more information. I called and made an appointment to provide my testimony to a priest at the Dioceses of Harrisburg. I was nervous. I can't stress enough that I am *not* Catholic. Even though I had Catholic friends my entire life, the Catholic Church always seemed a little scary and strange to me. Priests are even scarier. I was convinced priests were given the power to read minds, and if I met one he would know about me having sex with my Catholic college boyfriend, with whom I had no intention of getting married or making babies, the countless pro-choice marches I attended in college, and the fact that I tend to instantly befriend virtually anyone who is gay.

I felt certain that I was about to become a hostile defendant in a trial with a scary, judgmental priest cross-examining me. This was quite a few years ago when an intense German guy was the Pope, not like today with a cool Latin American dude running things in Rome.

In the fall of 2009 I drove to Harrisburg and found the enormous Diocese of Harrisburg complex. I walked inside the vast lobby and up to a stiff receptionist who was sitting behind bullet proof glass. No lie, *bullet proof glass*. She handed me a badge and provided directions to the Tribunal floor. I had to be buzzed through a series of locked doors to get there. I was not easily intimidated but, *damn*, this place was scary.

I gave my name to the Tribunal secretary and waited in the hallway for the priest. I already had a set mental image. He would be tall and thin, with dark hair and a black robe. He would be very serious and have no time for witticisms, sarcasm, or laughter of any sort. I also assumed he would judge me and hate me instantly as I was sooooo not Catholic.

Eventually the priest appeared in the doorway. He

was a large, jolly man with thinning gray hair and an enormous smile. He put out his giant hand to shake mine and invited me into his office. I liked him immediately. I sat in my chair already feeling completely relieved and comfortable.

"I read your letter," he said, "and it was very helpful. Before we begin, I need to tell you something important. If there is one thing I cannot stand in this world it is a liar."

Oh, thank you God, he gets it, was my immediate thought.

"I have a tape recorder because my memory isn't always perfect, and this way I can play it back later in case I forget something important. You can ask me to turn it off at any time if there is something you don't want on the record."

I thanked him and assured him there was nothing I needed to hide or would choose not to have recorded. He pushed the button and we began the most therapeutic interaction I'd had since discovering my ex's online profile. I should never have gone to therapy after the divorce. I could have made an appointment at the Diocese of Harrisburg and saved a ton of time and money.

I explained that I was not testifying to prevent the

annulment. In many ways, I was in favor of the annulment and I felt comfortable leaving the decision up the Tribunal. What I was in fact denying was my ex's claim that the marriage had dissolved because I had taken birth control. Yes, I had taken birth control, but it was a choice we'd made together. We were not Catholic and did not feel ready for children. More importantly, my ex had told me many times that he was not sure he ever wanted children at all. He said it often enough I worried we never would have children. At the same time, this was not something I would have considered a huge conflict in our relationship, and it certainly wasn't the reason for the divorce.

I went on to explain, in detail, the real reason I'd kicked him out of our home and filed for divorce. Before I was finished the priest stopped me and asked, "Wait, you mean he didn't mention infidelity or lying as part of the reason for the annulment? Are you sure?"

"It wasn't on any of the paperwork I received."

"Wait, here, I'm going to check all the paperwork we have on file."

He stopped the recorder and left the room. He returned a few minutes later with an angry look on his face and flipped the recorder back on.

"It isn't on any of his paperwork. Nothing about

lying or cheating."

"Would it have hurt him in this process if he had included it?" I asked.

"No! It would have helped! He's only telling us a small part of the truth and leaving out the important things. He needs counseling. This also may explain why you beat him in here. He hasn't even made his appointment to testify yet."

I finished the rest of my story, and once again felt the need to explain my presence at the Diocese. "I don't want to fight this. It's just so clear to me that he's still lying. If he's going to get married again, the only way it will last is if he stops this pattern. I know it could seem like I'm just here to cause problems for him, but that isn't the case. The lying in our relationship was devastating, and I would hate to see another woman go through it."

After the business end of my visit was through, we talked for at least 20 more minutes. We knew some of the same people from my time as a student teacher in the local Catholic high school. It was a fun and relaxing conversation. He thanked me for my time and testimony. He told me that the annulment would most likely go through but not without a tremendous amount of effort and counseling on my ex's part.

I was a little sad I would have no reason to see the

priest again. In a different time and place I could see how we would have totally been friends. While annulments still seem like a loophole to me, I also began to view them as a second chance for people. By deeply investigating what went wrong in a past relationship, perhaps couples had a better chance the second time around. The priest I met that day didn't seem to be just a cog in a machine meant to bring more money and more Catholics back to the church. He seemed to really care about the process and the people. It was not at all what I expected from a practice so shrouded in secrecy.

The day was powerful for a different reason. Over the years I was able to witness how people with damage, people with unresolved issues, could hurt not only themselves, but others as well. My time and energy spent on the annulment was not meant to be a retaliation against my ex. I knew he was going to be awarded the annulment eventually. My testimony was an attempt to get him have his dishonesty and his dysfunctional method of operation openly questioned. To make him confront the real reason our relationship had crumbled. I was also hoping to give his next partner and his next marriage a chance.

That day, I started to see that through my ability to understand human behavior—the way people feel and operate—I could have a positive impact. I not only slayed another dragon, defeated another villain, I had emerged from the battle stronger than before. Each time I stood up for myself, and did so in a positive way, it became like physical therapy for my soul. I could not fully become a super hero until I not only learned to appreciate my powers, but also heal from the wounds of the past.

Chapter 29

The first year of my children's lives was mostly about survival. All infants are delicate to a degree. Premature children, even months after they are born, are more so. When Gabby came home from the hospital she had a heart monitor strapped to her for two months. If that isn't an indication of fragility I don't know what is.

There are tons of potential fatalities infants must overcome. Car seats must never face the front of the vehicle. Babies can die quietly in their sleep if placed on their stomachs. Changing tables, if used improperly, become the source of severe head trauma or even death. Toys and candy, if small enough, are not fun or sweet; they are choking hazards. Don't even get me started on the many dangers of bathing. The added element of the prematurity of my kids meant every germ, every visitor with a sniffle, was as deadly as a loaded gun sitting on my coffee table.

My kids survived all of that only to become hazardously mobile. Toddlers do not understand danger, nor do they understand most verbal commands. They are like drunk frat boys skipping around the edge of a roof on a high-rise building.

So, I transformed my house into a gated community. The stairs and access points were all fitted with a series of barriers and fences. All sharp or delicate objects were taken to the attic. Some are still there. I would visit the homes of other families with toddlers and note the minimum-security status of their gate systems. With multiple children on the move I had no choice but to take the Alcatraz approach. At the same time, I also was slowly losing my security staff.

Understandably, I no longer needed as many people to help me with my kids as I did when they were in the infant stage. Toddlers sleep more, are easier to feed, and simply don't need the near constant care babies do. Most of my army had gone beyond the call of duty, and it was time for them to move on. I couldn't rely on the kindness of relatives and friends forever.

I had mixed feelings about becoming a more independent mother. It was good to have my own space back. While I had grown to accept and even like having people around most of the time, my default setting was still to be on my own. I was the type of person who needed time alone, away from the noise and messages I heard and felt from others. It also made my life feel a little more normal to not have a house full of people every day.

On the other hand, I was nervous. Toddlers still

require a lot of work and energy. This was another stage of life I had little if any experience in supporting. I just wanted to do it right. Even though they had survived the perilous first year, they still seemed very fragile. It felt like I could still really screw things up.

As the children progressed from infants to toddlers —from sweet, wiggly, non-verbal blobs to walking, talking beings with energy and personality—life became more interesting, more colorful, and a bit scarier. More than once I had a thought that froze me in my tracks: "crap, they are people now."

What helped quite a bit was the fact that as infants, and as toddlers, they were just so damn cute. Blond hair, big eyes, and the sweetest little smiles. They were also so cuddly. Even back at the hospital, when they were tiny little preemies, the nurses would talk about how unusually snuggly they were. I've heard, more than once, this theory that God makes babies and toddlers cute, so we don't leave them out on the curb. It is so true. I could be so wiped out after work, completely overwhelmed, and then I'd give a bath to my kids, look at those pinch-able little butts, and all would be well with the world.

If I felt like I knew nothing about raising infants and toddlers, I felt like I knew even less about raising boys. I knew about girls. I had been teaching only teenage girls for over ten years when my kids were born. Little boys, with their boy parts, fart jokes, and their wrestly energy were such incomprehensible things.

I certainly wasn't prepared for how sweet little boys can be. How extra super cuddly they were. My little boys were also so curious about life. They loved museums, books, nature, and learning how things were made and fit together.

One day when he was around three or so, Charlie was running a high fever and I had to take him, late in the evening, to the pediatrician. She gave us a prescription and sent us to a 24-hour pharmacy. It took forever. Charlie was sick and tired, but also a little bored. While we waited, I took him to the small rack of toys for sale in the store. I told him he could have anything he wanted because he was being such a trooper. He chose a kid's anatomy book written probably for 10-year olds. I kept asking him if he was sure. Didn't he want a matchbox car or a dinosaur? For years Charlie read and re-read that book until it literally fell apart.

Around age four I took Anthony on a school field trip with me to The University of Pennsylvania's Museum of Anthropology. He not only sat through a 45-minute lecture about mummification, given by one of the U Penn professors, he asked questions during the Q and A period.

He had more patience and was more focused during the presentation than some of my students.

My boys could still be "regular" boys. They would laugh and roll around on the floor together until one of them cried. They loved to pee in the potty at the exact same time. They went through an obsession with construction equipment and pretty much anything with wheels. One time, we attended a tractor parade near my parent's vacation cabin. Literally just a line of tractor after tractor driving slowly in front of a small, rural crowd. When I tried to get us out of there, because I was bored out of my skull, they cried until we sat back down and watched the rest of it. Every blessed tractor.

Meanwhile, Gabby was turning in to her own little person as well. Gabby became the happiest little soul you can imagine. She saw the world through a permanent pair of rose colored glasses. Very little got her down. In many ways, she was also a girly girl. Tutus, pink, the whole nine yards.

Gabby was no delicate little flower, though. Sweet and positive, but always tough. She never had a first word; she had a first phrase: "I do it." She wasn't afraid to let her brothers know if they were being unfair or not doing the right thing. More than once I saw her lay in to an older boy at the park if he took her ball or tried to take her swing, only moments later to skip away sweetly and play in the sand. She was never interested in becoming a princess, because she was born a queen.

Even though I was nervous about raising them, I found that what I most needed to do was love them and appreciate them for who they were. Not to put expectations on them or try to change them. I don't remember feeling a ton of love as a child, and that was something I knew I could provide for them. I didn't have a big house, and they didn't even have a father, but I had my love and that had to be enough. Toys can be broken, houses can burn down. Love and acceptance sticks with us all of our lives, and is much harder to find in the big bad real world. The more I could give my kids early on, the better chance they would have to hold on to it.

Chapter 30

During the almost two years after Chris died, the holidays in my house were busy and filled with friends and family at every moment. I could feel the love everywhere. On the third Christmas morning without Chris, I woke up alone. My parents came over because everyone else had plans, and I had three two-year olds to play with. The kids still didn't fully understand Christmas. They just liked to play with the wrapping paper and boxes. For me it was sort of, well, sad. It was one of many moments when my heart ached for another person.

At 36 years I had spent over a third of my life in some form of a committed relationship. I had been married or partnered for most of my adult life. I never felt like I needed a man, but it was always comforting, even when it was bad. Companionship made life feel more balanced somehow. So being alone was hard at times. Even with a house full of kids it could feel lonely, especially at night when they were asleep.

As the kids were growing up I worried about the fact that there were few regular male figures in their lives. I know tons of women who have successfully raised kids without fathers. I wasn't desperate for them to have a new one. After two years "alone" we were still doing fine. The kids were not difficult children. I still had quite a few regular helpers, so I had more support than most moms. It was also sort of nice to have ultimate power over decisions concerning them. I never had to "check" with a spouse; I just decided what was best for them and accepted the consequences. Yet, I still wasn't ready to give up on love for myself, or on finding a potential father figure for them.

I dated a few more people with varying degrees of failure. I discovered that divorced or single men in their late 30's and early 40's are often completely ill equipped to date properly. My experience consisted of men who were either completely freaked out by my situation and/or my past, or men who freaked me out for any variety of reasons.

Some guys were a little too eager to jump right in to my family. One proposed within three weeks. Others seemed barely able to take care of themselves, let alone a family. One guy, on a Christian site, sent one nice, normal message, then filled the next one with sexually explicit stuff. I had to be choosier than I had been before becoming a mother. When it was just me, I could convince myself to focus on the good and overlook red flags. I used to use my sensitivity on dates to peer deeply into a guy's soul; the new me used my power to screen potential problem relationships.

The weird part was that I liked dating. I know, I know, tons of people don't like dating. But I really did. I liked getting to know people. I liked eating in restaurants. I liked talking. I also really loved the first kiss thing. Those situations where you think you feel a spark but aren't sure the other person does. Sitting across from them, wondering what they are thinking. Wondering if this is a friendship thing or if the guy secretly wants to aggressively push aside his plate of vindaloo and rice, and ravage me right there in the Taste of India to the sounds of sitar music and sizzling meat.

Later, maybe by the car or outside of a residence, the true moment arrives. The one where I know if it is going to happen, it must happen now. My lips tingling from the spicy dinner, I might touch his coat a little as I thank him for the lovely evening. Hopefully, he leans in closer and bam, it happens. Lips touch, arms wrap around bodies, hands maybe move around a bit, and it just feels exciting, and oh so good. The beautiful moment of making out for the first time with a cute guy is awesome.

"I'm too tired. I just don't feel like it. He isn't even that interested. What is the point?"

All of this is my complaint to my friend Mary Lou. She had agreed to take care of my now two-year old triplets as I went on yet another first date.

Mary Lou loved my family so much. Years before, she had heard through the town information super highway that someone needed help with their triplets. She called my sister and eagerly volunteered her services. She remained a faithful Wednesday night child helper for years after others had moved on. We were at the point where she kept coming because I needed her friendship and support more than the kids did. Her first marriage had been rocky, so she completely understood my wish to find a good guy to spend some time with. She morphed from stranger to super hero sidekick in no time.

I kept viewing it as one last ditch effort, but it felt as if I'd made at least 365 last ditch efforts at dating. Dating was getting stale, and so was my enthusiasm. However, Mary Lou encouraged me to go anyway. She was excited to babysit and thought a night out would be good for me. After all, it was only for coffee. I hesitantly agreed and headed into the city of Lancaster in my minivan. I always felt like an ass going on a first date in my minivan.

I met Craig on Match.Com. It was inexpensive, and members could look through profiles and use their own good judgment about choosing individuals to wink at or message. I kept my profile hidden and chose to limit my potential suitors to those I contacted first. This was partially because I had young children at home and didn't want creeps or serial killers to find me, and because I felt like I knew practically every single resident within a 40-mile radius of my home. If I had a viewable profile, it would take only minutes for the entire county to find out the Widow Billett was on the prowl yet again.

Craig's profile was simple and straightforward. He was a college mathematics professor, who liked good music and appreciated the arts. One must be smart to be a Doctor of Mathematics, and smart was always say sexier than muscles in my book. He was also tall and good looking in an 1840's kind of way. I figured, what the hell.

I sent him a little message and in a day or so he sent a message back. He was new to the area and had just started working at a local college. His messages were short and to the point. I could not get a good read on his sense of humor, interest in me, or even much of his personality. When he asked if I wanted to meet for coffee I was more curious than interested.

When I arrived at the coffee house he was waiting outside. He was tall, slim, and nicely dressed. He had thick, dark hair, and these interesting side burns in a time before hipster guys had taken facial hair to the ZZ Top level. He paid for our drinks and we sat outside. About 15 minutes into our conversation a barista poked her head out the door and told us the cafe would be closing in five minutes. I was a little embarrassed by my native city. Only in Lancaster could a city coffee shop close at 8pm. It was barely even dark.

After being kicked off the coffee shop sidewalk we chose to go for a walk through the city. Craig had literally just moved there, and I'd lived near or in the city for many years. So, I was a pretty good walking tour-guide. It turned out to be a nice comfortable way to have a conversation. I learned more about him, and of course I babbled about myself. When the date ended I gave him a hug and he promised to be in touch. He seemed nice, and I chalked it up to a decent date with a decent guy.

I cannot remember the exact details of how our relationship progressed after the first date. What I do know is we were both fairly reserved at first and took things slowly. Eventually, we would get into a dating routine. On Tuesday evenings, Craig would visit me at my house after the kids went to bed, and we would watch a movie and have a snack together. On Friday nights, we would go out to dinner. It was a very comfortable little relationship and we always had a nice time. He was a southern gentleman. Meaning, he opened car doors for me and paid for our dates. While my appreciation of this may make some feminists want to roll their eyes or scream, after all I had been through, if ANYONE, male, female, Martian, etc… wanted to open a door for me or buy me a meal, I was completely cool with it.

I was very careful not to rush anything with Craig. For months, I deliberately kept our lives separate. Work LuAnn could focus on career, Mommy LuAnn could focus on family, and Dating LuAnn got to have a little fun and relax twice a week. It was humming along perfectly until Craig and I both started to develop stronger feelings for one another. It was getting harder for him to leave after our twice weekly dates, and it was getting harder to say goodbye.

I knew eventually he would need to meet my kids, and I was a little nervous about this. Craig came off as a bit reserved much of the time. While he was comfortable and funny around me, I could not really picture him being comfortable around kids. Craig was a pretty quiet, organized guy. My boys bounced between being intellectuals and tractor pull enthusiasts. Gabby was simply a ball busting flurry of pink. He tried to explain he was the oldest of four and was used to children, but I just couldn't picture this reserved math professor with the confederate side burns rolling around at the park with my kids.

Finally, I had to face the situation and bring the four together. And it turned out Craig was amazing with them. He was funny and sweet, and the kids seemed drawn to him. He got down on the floor and played games with them, but at the same time he did not push anything. He allowed them to come to him and wanted them to really control the interaction. I was shocked and amazed, and my feelings for Craig deepened.

Our relationship blossomed in what felt like a very natural and comfortable way starting the first night when we were ejected from the coffee shop. We would eventually move from seeing one another two times a week to three times a week. A month or so later we would add another day. By the time summer arrived, Craig was spending less time in his townhouse and more time at my house.

Being in a relationship with a college professor was perfect, schedule-wise. My boarding school teaching job tended to follow a collegiate schedule, so often we would have the same time off from work. Like me, Craig had the entire summer free. He joined the kids and me at the pool, at the park, and in the back yard. The best part was I suddenly had a man around the house.

Craig was not your stereotypical math geek. He

could fix almost anything: cars, washing machines, furniture, etc... He also played the guitar and sang. He was fun to have around, entertaining, supportive, and he even took out the trash. He would drive to my house from his apartment on Wednesday evenings just to take my garbage to the curb for the Thursday morning pickup. He did this without expecting or wanting any sort of recognition. My father, by counterexample, is disappointed when my mother does not literally jump up and down and praise him for vacuuming the carpet. My father would do very well in some sort of pre-school chore chart sticker program. Craig, on the other hand, took on many chores around my house with quiet humility.

After spending enough time with Craig and my family combined, I discovered Craig's spirit animal: the border collie. His natural instinct is to organize and protect the herd. He can do so in a very calm, very natural way. Like a herding dog, he does not do this for praise. He protects his charges because it is what he was born to do, and he is happiest when he is fulfilling his duty. If bats and spiders can be super heroes, so can dogs. Craig is my Border Collie Man.

I worried that when the summer ended, so would this easy relationship with this super guy. My dream relationship used to involve sexy, exciting times with carefree mornings and long dinners at fancy restaurants. Very Danielle Steele meets Anastasia Steele. Craig did not ride up on a white horse, but instead rolled up in a tan, dented, mid-90's Mercury Sable sedan. This relationship with Craig was the true, realistic dream. He was a handsome, smart, funny man who wanted to support my family and I, without an exhausting need for intense displays of gratitude.

I had been through enough in my life to know I should not or would not take this relationship for granted. I was careful to guard myself as much as possible. Craig's job at the University was temporary. He was a visiting professor, which meant that although he was full time, with full pay and full benefits for two years, there was no guarantee he would be offered an extension or a permanent job. In fact, because he was covering for a professor who was on an extended sabbatical, the chance of the job lasting more than two years was nearly impossible. Jobs at the college were too good. Professors stayed on until they almost literally had to be carried out on stretchers.

I quickly learned that professors do not often stay in one place while looking for a tenure track position. Professors are different from teachers, in that professors tend to follow the jobs. Often those jobs are not anywhere close to one's previous job. Craig had only had his PHD for a month when we first met, so he was necessarily as experienced as other applicants, and would need to look for work wherever a position in mathematics was available.

About a year after we started dating he began searching for his next position. He sent resumes to colleges and universities all over the country. While he wanted to stick close to Pennsylvania or his home state, Virginia, the reality was that if he were going to further his career, he would have to accept the best offer regardless of location.

This scared the crap out of me. While he did not have a strong connection to any place, I had thick, deep roots in Lancaster County. My job of close to 15 years was in the Lancaster area. My family, my friends, and most importantly, my free childcare was in Lancaster. I was not in a place to pull up stakes and toddlers and move to hell knows where. Craig was also not at a point where he could support a new family in a new place if I didn't have a job or support.

The kids were still young. This motherhood thing was still new. I felt like I needed the familiar, the parts of life I knew and could count on to ground me. On the surface I was this independent, single Mom. Underneath it all I still had a vast network of support. I just couldn't comprehend functioning well without it. I needed more than just my skills of time management and sensitivity to survive.

We discussed this tricky situation and came to the conclusion that he would have to follow the jobs and we would most likely have to keep up some sort of long distance relationship. Perhaps, after a year or two when we were both strong financially we could talk about moving. The only downside was I couldn't imagine wanting to move to another state even if we had oil drums full of money.

I did what I always do in seemingly no win, no chance situations. I prayed my guts out. I prayed all of the time. Usually, I prayed for guidance or for God to just show me what was right and what was best. Not in this case. In this case, I prayed for God to help Craig land a job close to my town and keep this amazing man in our lives. And I did not mean in our lives but three states away.

Early in Craig's job search I had a suspicion that God was on my side in this situation. As letters and responses started coming in, Craig said to me, "Why does it seem like only schools in Pennsylvania are interested in me? I apply everywhere, but I only get responses and interviews from schools 'close to your house?"

I just smiled and told him I had no idea.

When his job at Franklin and Marshall was coming to an end, a State University in Pennsylvania about an hour and half from my house offered him a job. It was not a great position, but it was a solid offer and Craig took it. He rented an apartment halfway between my home and the campus and spent approximately 12 full nights total in the apartment during the full years' time he was renting.

I was happy, but still worried. Craig quickly discovered this state university job was not ideal and immediately restarted his job search. He finished out a full year at the school but had no desire to stay even though the school wanted him to. The University was small and didn't have good resources. The pay was not great, a number of his colleagues were chain-smoking grumps, and many of the students were unmotivated. It was far from his dream job. I had to pray again and pray harder. I did not want him to move away.

Chapter 31

If you ever really want to drive me over the edge, make me wait or waste my time. To say my time is precious seems so arrogant, but my time is very precious. Almost every moment is carefully accounted for and filled with some form of useful activity. Often, I'll make the most of my time by constructing ways to achieve multiple goals at once. On any given day, you might find me reading an important document while simultaneously bathing a child, doing laundry, cleaning the bathroom, and baking oatmeal. If any of this book seems disconnected it might be because I was writing parts of it between classes at work while chatting with a parent on the phone and making photocopies for the incoming class. This may be no different from the multi-tasking performed by most mothers, but I for one embrace it. I secretly live for extreme multi-tasking. It gives me a sick little rush.

It might be another super power, a coping mechanism, or hell even a compulsion. I don't know if it's a good or bad thing. It is simply how I function. Not only do I multi-task, I do practically everything in my life as quickly as I can. And I can do things—laundry, lesson plans, even shopping—really, really fast.

I want to be careful not to give the impression that I'm this total wiz at balance or someone who never gets overwhelmed. Far from it. One autumn in particular, things were coming to a head. Work was busier than ever, I was trudging through the pre-coursework for an upcoming graduate school intensive, and I was stressed out beyond belief. I finally just had to sit down and pray. I prayed to God to help me. I was in over my head and could see no end to the stress.

God answered my prayer almost immediately in an unexpected way. He broke my arm.

It was Gretna Day which is a special, yearly surprise picnic and roller skating party event at the school where I teach. I was roller skating with my students and laughing with my teacher friends. I enjoyed this particular activity very much. I was a good skater and hadn't even had a minor fall on my tush in over a decade.

I was blissfully skating along when bam, a student fell right in front of me. I had to make a split-second decision. Run over the poor girl or take the fall. I took the fall and I took it hard.

The pain was almost blinding. I had heard the saying, "you know it like the back of your hand" many times. Well, I knew the back of my hand and this hand was not mine. It was immediately a swollen, deformed, mangled lump of skin and fingers. A moment later, I passed out.

When I woke up I was skate-less, flat on my back, with my legs propped up on the school nurse. I was still on the rink floor and students were whizzing on by. Occasionally, one would stop and say, "Ms. Billett, are you okay?"

Of course, I'm okay! I do this all the time. I love laying on a hard, dirty floor with my legs in the air!

I just wanted to get the hell out of there. The nurse and some teachers asked if I could walk, and we made it close to the edge of the rink before I passed out again. When I woke up I was a little closer to the exit, again on the floor, legs back on the nurse. Dammit. This time when I tried to stand up the adults wouldn't let me.

"The ambulance is on its way."

My colleagues talked to me and kept me company while we waited. They said kind things like, "Maybe you are getting a little too old to skate," and "You know, you aren't a teenager anymore."

A kid fell in front of me. What was I supposed to do, jump over her?

Eventually, the paramedics arrived and loaded me onto a stretcher. It was humiliating being rolled out of the skating rink in front of over 200 teenage girls. My friend Jen followed behind in her car with my purse and shoes. I was hoping she managed to pick up my ego, too, as I most certainly left it inside the rink.

As I waited in the ER Jen arrived at my side. "I found your phone and I called your parents, Craig, MiMi, Shane, and anyone else I could think of. I told them you probably broke your arm and you passed out a bunch of times. Wow, your arm looks horrible. It has to be broken. Like, really broken. Oh my God, how many unread text messages do you have? Hey, some of these are from me! How many un-heard voice-mails are on this thing? Some of them are from me too! What the hell LuAnn, do you ever actually use your phone?"

She continued to invade my cellular privacy until the Doctor finally came in.

"That looks pretty bad. What did you do? *Roller Skating*? Well, you aren't a teenager anymore."

Thanks, Doc.

Jen addressed the doctor with authority. "It has got to be broken. She needs morphine and maybe some heavy narcotics to take home. She gets sick on most other pain killers, so try for one that won't make her nauseous. Drug her up Doctor, she is in a lot of pain."

Thanks, Jen.

He actually listened to her completely amateur medical advice and ordered some morphine. Later he would write out a pain med prescription. Normally, I would be little concerned about a doctor listening to a fast-talking riding instructor whose medical expertise was limited to a degree in equine science, but the morphine was lovely, lovely stuff. Jen rose to the level of patient advocate goddess in my fuzzy mind.

After a short blissful wait, I was sent into the X-ray room. "Ouch!" winced the tech from behind the X-ray room glass. "Ugh!" said the other one.

"Are you looking at my X ray?" I asked in a small voice. "Is it broken?"

I heard a chuckle, "Um, I'll let the doctor make the final assessment, but yah it looks pretty broken."

Jen passed the time taking photos of me and sending them to people via my phone. Finally, the doctor came back later and showed me my X-ray. There are eight bones in a human wrist that connect the arm to the hand. All eight of mine were pushed up and scattered in different directions. The doctor explained that he and a colleague would have to set it. He said it would feel a lot better after it was set, but the numbing process could be a bit painful. He wasn't kidding. The injection was so excruciating I almost passed out again. Numbness was successfully achieved however, and he and another doctor set the bones.

The next day I went to an orthopedic doctor and was told that even though the bones were set, they may not stay that way. He gave me a couple options. I could keep the arm in a cast for six weeks and hope there was no shifting of bones, or I could choose to undergo surgery. Surgery would involve inserting a metal plate in my arm and screwing it to the bones. The recovery would be tougher initially, but I would get the use of my arm back much faster. "Use of my arm fast" was all I needed to hear, and I opted for surgery.

Afterward, I had to stay home from work for about two weeks. I was forced to cancel my intensive course and put it off until the spring. Multi-tasking was out of the question. Doing things quickly was also impossible. Even going to the bathroom was a challenge and took tons of time.

I was forced to lie in bed for most of the day with my arm in the air. I thought the arm in the air thing was stupid until my hand swelled up like a punching balloon. I started following doctor's orders after that. The pain pills left me so loopy I couldn't even concentrate enough to read. Essentially, I could eat, watch tv, and sleep. God had answered my prayers. I was bored out of my mind but felt no stress.

Luckily, some of the people who had helped when the triplets were young stepped back in to help again. I could literally do nothing productive. The kids were so sweet. They would visit me and carefully climb in my bed. They would bring me little toys and make me smile.

It was important to observe that my world could continue without me. I had help again with the kids. The tons of tasks I normally performed at work were picked up by colleagues. It became clear that while I put such enormous pressure on myself, by letting a few things go, I could still have an intact family and job.

I wish I could say that after I recovered and returned to my normal life, I was able to completely slow down and avoid stress. I'd learned a lesson, but I was still me. Approximately two years after God broke my arm, he gave me an infection in my appendix. It was another time when I was doing too much and needed a wakeup call. Emergency surgery and a few weeks of recovery got the message through. While this overextending myself is quite likely part of my DNA, I do keep myself in check in a more careful way. I now know that when I overdo it, God will put me in the hospital. So, I try to chill out before he feels compelled to strike me down.

Chapter 32

"Kids, how would you feel about your mother and I getting married?" Craig asked my three little ones.

"Yay, great! When will you start having babies?"

Craig and I both smiled. Things were finally falling into place, and it was time for us to unite as a family.

At the end of his final semester at the state university, Penn State offered him a full-time teaching job at their Harrisburg campus a mere 45-minute highway commute from my house. Penn State is not really a state school. It is semi-private, taking some state assistance, but privately endowed for the most part. This translates into more money, better benefits, and broader resources. Craig eagerly accepted the great position, and we began to talk about a wedding.

At first, we considered just eloping at a justice of the peace or even Las Vegas, and simply making the marriage official. It was Craig, however, who expressed a desire for the children to be part of it. One day he said to me, "You know, I'm not just marrying you, I'm marrying your kids too. Do you think they should be involved in the wedding?"

"I don't know. Why don't we ask them?"

Talking to the kids is my preferred approach when deciding on non-crucial things that affect the family like which restaurant to go to or if a new movie looks like something they might be interested in. I value the opinions of my children, and they are happy to share them. At the same time, I'm not an idiot. I don't ask them if they would like to get vaccinations, or how they feel about teeth brushing and regular school attendance. I'm not one to let my inmates totally run the asylum.

Together, Craig and I brought up the idea of being part of our wedding, and they unanimously agreed. In many ways, Craig was the only father they have ever known. He had been with them through potty training, the transition from cribs to beds, the first day of pre-school, and the first lost teeth. Sometimes when the kids were scared or hurt, they would call out to Craig before they would yell for me. It is okay, because quite honestly, he'd get there faster. I could not imagine a better man for the job.

We decided to keep the wedding as small as possible. We found a little bed and breakfast near Gettysburg that advertised elopement weddings. For less than a thousand dollars we could have an officiant, a cake, flowers, two nights in the B&B, and six guests. Sold.

A few people were a little miffed they weren't

invited, but we didn't really care. Craig had been married before, and I'd been married twice. As excited as I was to marry Craig, I was still a little self-conscious about the fact this was my third wedding. I mean, come on, I'm not Elizabeth Taylor. Hell, I'm not even Brittany Spears. I always knew I would not lead an ordinary life, but at the same time I never thought I would be needing a separate closet for my wedding dresses.

That summer morning marked the first time in a long time, maybe in my entire life, where I felt whole, comfortable, and relaxed. Craig was my soft place to land at the end of the day, and after a few short words, he became that soft place until death do us part. After so many years of surviving on strength and sheer will, it was unbelievably nice to be an official part of a strong team.

Chapter 33

When it was time for my kids to start school, around age 3, I signed them up for the pre-school located in the church I was attending. It was a fabulous program with caring, qualified adults, and a solid curriculum. Most importantly, they were happy there. They attended a few days a week for three hours a day. The rest of the time relatives and friends would watch them at home until I returned from work.

I decided early on to do my best to find the correct school for my kids. Because of what I had been reading about state educational standards and public-school curriculum that focused mainly on standardized tests, I had concerns. I taught in a private school where we were accredited but were not required to follow Pennsylvania state standards. The result? High SAT scores, AP scores, and 100% college placement after graduation. I knew first hand that the right private school could provide not only a solid education but also foster a love of school and learning.

I considered how much of a child's day is spent in school. When one counts waking hours only, kids are at school more than at home. It was important for me to find a place where my kids could be happy to learn and grow both academically and socially. Not every child could find that balance in the 21st century American public-school system.

My parents were worried. Private school, even when one qualifies for financial aid, can be expensive. Pennsylvania has descent public schools, so why would I pay for something we could get for free? Public school had been fine for their kids, and we all turned out okay.

It is true, public school was fine when I attended it. I also went to school before the days of No Child Left Behind and State funding for schools based on test scores. I attended public school when arts programs, electives, field trips, and recess weren't being cut to make way for more test preparation. This option no longer seemed so fine. When adults look for important things, places to live, houses, jobs, I doubt that *decent* or *okay* is what they really want. Most want the best they can afford and the best they can get.

Because I am an educator and good is not good enough when it comes to educating my kids, the decision was not hard for me at all. I could live in a smaller house, drive a used van, take simple trips instead of elaborate vacations, and cut out anything unnecessary so I could afford to give my children something I consider more important.

For kindergarten, I chose to keep my children in their Christian school. The pre-school program was so solid that I figured the elementary classes would be good too. That part was correct. It turned out the educational program at the Christian school was superior to the kindergarten program in the local public school. It was however, not as good as the pre-school program had been. The kindergarten teacher was older and seemed a little overwhelmed. My kids found her assistant teacher grouchy, and she used poor grammar. It was a small class, which was nice, but there were some unkind, borderline bullies. Because the school was so small, the mean children could possibly be their classmates for the remainder of their academic career. My kids would also be together all the time. I was worried they wouldn't gain independence or make close friends if they were never divided.

My three had a reputation for being well behaved. We received very few notes or messages about conflict or misbehavior. So, I was surprised when, at an early conference, the kindergarten teacher raised concerns about Gabby.

"Gabby has been falling off her chair on purpose during lessons. She does not seem to want to focus at times. Punishments don't seem to bother her. I think you should consider having her tested for ADHD."

Gabby, the girl I had taken to a three-hour dance recital where she sat quietly engaged the entire time? Gabby, the girl I could take to a fine dining restaurant where she could enjoy the meal and conversation like a mini adult? Gabby, who could entertain herself for hours with just one activity? I had taken this kid to meetings when I couldn't find a sitter, and she always sat quietly coloring during conversations that were super boring, even to me.

I am not one to think, "Oh no, not my child!" However, I have also worked with students with ADHD, and I did not witness in her the behaviors and tendencies I had seen in my ADHD students. Then it hit me, all the women in Gabby's life were strong women. Loving, caring, but firm. Gabby didn't respect this teacher. The lady was older, seemed overwhelmed, and didn't command respect like most of the women Gabby was used to. She was goofing around because she didn't recognize this woman was in charge.

I knew I couldn't change this teacher, and I also knew I wasn't going to run off and get Gabby tested. She was six. I did, however, begin to look more critically at the teachers in the grades above Kindergarten. The first-grade teacher did not seem much better.

The final nail in the coffin for the little school happened during a book fair. I volunteered as a person who would help the preschoolers choose books. The kids would point out books they were interested in, I would write down the titles on a card, and the card would be sent home to their parents. If the parents chose, they could buy some, none, or all the books the child had chosen. It was fun for the kids, and the parents had ultimate control over what was purchased.

One of the other parent volunteers called me over to her, where a cute little blond pre-school boy stood at her side.

"He wants a Fancy Nancy book. I don't think I should put that on the card."

I was taken completely off guard.

"Why not?" I said, doing my best to hold back my building anger. "Just write it down and the parents will decide if they want to buy it for him."

In no time other moms came over to give their two cents. Yes, the little boy was still right there, listening.

"I wouldn't want my son to get a Fancy Nancy book," one woman said, and several others nodded in agreement.

I was not only livid, I was the only one in the room

who seemed to realize this line of thinking was completely ridiculous. I did not want my children to attend a school where kids were discouraged from reading ANY kind of book. What were these women worried about? That Fancy Nancy was part of an underground conspiracy to turn little boys gay?!! In my own home there were tons of every kind of book including Nancy and her fanciness. Truck books, princess books, animal books, you name it! My children could pick up any book to read, or request any book to be read to them.

Boys leave the room because I'm going to read something to Gabby from that fag hag Pinkaliscious! Don't want you turning all homo on me! Gabby, go to your room, I'm going to put on Bob the Builder for your brothers. Don't want you to become some spanish speaking, tool belt sporting lesbian!

I could not send my children to a school with kids who were bullies and adults who felt empowered to be openly judgmental. Many parents have their "thing." Some need their kids to attend a school with a super healthy lunch program. Others might focus on the quality of the sports teams or technology. My thing is how the school community treats one another, and how the families teach their kids to treat others. It isn't only my mom thing, it's my super hero thing. Protecting people, especially kids, from mis-directed assumptions and opinions. If a child likes Fancy Nancy, for any reason, no one should feel it's okay to squash that. I didn't see their Christian school as an evil school, it was simply no longer the school for my family.

I consider myself a Christian. I believe strongly in God. I feel certain I would not have made it through most the of things I've survived without him. I also feel certain he helped save my Gabby when she had no amniotic fluid in the womb. I also believe in Jesus and his perfect life. And perfect included the way he supported and treated people, including those who were sinners.

I've noticed a change in the attitudes and behaviors of many Christians over the past decade or so. I feel and see a shift away from the model of Jesus. I feel anger from them and I hear their judgmental rhetoric. It seems to build and grow stronger every day. This collective vibe of judgement makes it very hard for me to be in large groups of Christian people. Their anger and criticism have become very difficult for me, as strong, negative emotions are still a struggle for me to bear.

I have a different way of seeing and defining sin from many in the religious right. I see sin as damage. We are born damaged and we hopefully spend our lives trying to fix some of the damage. We either win the war on our damage or let it overcome us. The word "sin" leads people to judge. The word "damage" should lead us to help each other heal. Jesus was perfect and without sin or damage, and all he wanted to do was bring people to his father and help them heal.

To me it isn't that hard to understand this concept. Behaviors considered sinful can stem from damage people have received at different times in their lives. The harm they get is often doled out to them by other damaged people. Sing begets sin, damage begets damage. What do I think Jesus would want us to do? Work on our own damage and help others to work on theirs. I do not think that means keeping kids from reading a book with a fancy female protagonist.

I had already been checking out a Montessori school in Lancaster city, about 20 minutes from where we lived. It was much larger than the Christian school, so there were three classes of each level, meaning my kids could be in separate classes and develop some independence. There were also tons of smart, caring, happy, open minded teachers and amazing families from a variety of races, religions, and socio-economic backgrounds. The common thread was that the families really cared about their children's education. While the Christian school had families like that too, there were also families who seemed to be using the Christian school to shelter their children from "the big bad secular world."

It wasn't going to be easy to change from the school my kids had been attending for years. There were teachers, administrators, and families they liked very much. The Montessori school was far more expensive. It would also involve putting the kids on a bus every day and sending them on a 30-45 minute ride both ways. Their current school was ten minutes away, and the public school was within walking distance from our home.

My parents thought I was insane. A more expensive school, in the city, with a long bus ride, when there were closer, cheaper schools that were perfectly good. *Perfectly good.* That was the problem. Good was not good enough for me, and especially not for my kids. I screwed up enough already. They didn't have their birth father. In many ways they never had a birth father. I just could not stand it if I fucked up their education.

So, starting in first grade we made the change. I sat them all down and said, "Your mother is an educator. You need to trust that I know what's is best for your education. I believe this new school is the right one for all of you. Many times, what is best is not what is easiest."

The transition was hardest on Anthony. When I bought a new refrigerator, it took him months to get over the loss of the old one. And he had way more invested in his school than the box that kept our food cold.

I believe I must have passed my sensitivity gene on to him. He is very in tune with the thoughts and feelings of others and feels them deeply. In the past he had always had his siblings with him, and he felt secure with them. In the new school he had trouble making friends at first. Kids would want to play with him, but he would get frustrated when they didn't want to play the things he wanted to play. He would also sense if a child was unsure about him or upset, which tended to hurt his feelings. From week one, the proactive classroom teachers at his school would watch him on the playground and talk to him about better ways to interact with other kids. His teachers recognized his sensitivity, worked with him on his struggles, and helped him find esteem in the things he was good at.

Within the first year he became a stronger kid. Still sensitive, but also one who loved school, had his friends over for playdates, and got invited to friends' houses often. He became better at dealing with change and worked through transitions more quickly than he used to. He even learned to love riding the bus! The school turned out to be worth every penny and every minor inconvenience.

Charles is sensitive too but has to a lesser degree. He handled the transition well, and quickly made friends. The first day of school he told everyone that he preferred to be called Charles instead of Charlie. It took some getting used to, but now he is Charles. Of all my kids he is the best at getting comfortable in new surroundings and making friends quickly. When I visit his school, I notice that some of the girls seem to have little crushes on him. He gets lots of hugs, and even gets chased on the playground. In many ways, he reminds me the most of his father. Sweet, thoughtful, smart, and clueless about the swarms of girls who adore him.

Gabby loved everything about her new school. She came home every day smiling. While she loves her brothers and plays well with them, she likes to have friends who are girls. School provides an opportunity to run around with her friends and be a bit girly. She is, however, the toughest of my three. If one of my children comes in the house muddy, or soaked, or with torn jeans, it will be Gabby 80% of the time. The girl is not afraid to play hard, even if she's in a dress.

Chapter 34

The fall 2014 school year began as they all have for the past 15 years of my life: exciting, chaotic, and familiar. However, I felt different.

Roughly a month into the school year I noticed I was getting grumpy, and some days I was full on anger while at my job. I wasn't angry at the students, but at the administration and all the thousands of tasks I had to tackle every day that went beyond my classroom work. The work load was not new or surprising. In fact, it was expected that every day I would multi task to the very edge, as well as tackle new challenges with energy and a smile. It took time to figure it out. The job was the same, but I was different.

For most of my professional life I'd been working to support myself, and at times other people. For well over a decade my job provided a place to live, precious health insurance, retirement, and most of all, stability. I worked at my job as if my life depended on it, because for all intents and purposes, it did. I rarely allowed myself the luxury of questioning the importance of working as hard as humanly possible.

It took months of crankiness for me to understand

what was going on. After years of loving my job like one loves a needy, demanding partner, I was starting to hate it. I hated the extra hours, I hated the extra tasks, I hated the pressure. These feelings scared me at first as I worried I was becoming a middle-aged anger management case.

Then I figured it out. It was all Craig's fault. By marrying Craig, I finally had something I'd honestly never had before in my adult life: security. Not only was Craig's job stable, but Craig himself was stable. While having this new-found rock of security in my life was wonderful, I was suddenly permitted to relax a bit. My old method of operation involved so many pieces, there had been little room for relaxation.

I was finally permitted the luxury of just doing a very good job. Not always stressing about things I couldn't handle. And more importantly, I could say "no" to requests and extra tasks. I did not have to work on every committee or assist with every club. It was hard at first to relax a bit at my job, but I think I became a better teacher when I no longer had to work from a place of worry.

The tragedy of losing Chris became like my own addict's rock bottom. It had forced me to re-evaluate how I was living my life, what was working and what was not. I could no longer squeak by on good enough; I'd needed to get my act together. Yet, in the process of becoming a fully functional working Mom, I'd lost the option of sinking back and enjoying life. Craig allowed me a sense of balance I may have never had before. When Craig came in to my life I was also able to stop blindly barreling forward through each stage of my children's lives; I could step aside sometimes and carefully evaluate my home life and my work life.

I've been working with teenage girls for over 18 years. I am one of those people who loves teenagers. I view their angst as understandable and temporary. The occasional moments of irrationality don't bother me. I see the amazing potential that all teenagers have. All of them. With the right guidance and support, I know these kids can become strong contributors to society. While I cannot help all of them, in my job I have a chance at giving them the support and guidance that might just push them past issues of insecurity, anger, and fear. Because I have been able to push past my own.

I know most of my students well and can tune in to their feelings. There is a difference between what it was like to experience this kind of thing from teenagers, and what it was like to sense the feelings of adults. When adults are angry, for example, I feel my own range of emotions from frustration and helplessness to disappointment.

Why are adults different than younger people? Why are adults harder? Because when I sense pain, I want to fix it. With adults, I might suspect I can't fix it. I might feel additional anxiety because the anger is generated toward me. I also might feel disgust because I can tell that person might never stop being angry. I've known people that have been angry for decades. My sensitive, understanding, helpful super hero side does not extend to negative adults like this. I either avoid them, or in some cases I confront them.

It is nearly unbearable to me when angry adults take out their frustrations on others, projecting their damage on innocent bystanders. Often, I just want to scream at them. I want to tell them I know how much life can suck, and moping around, or worse, making other people miserable, is not the way to feel better. Yet some of those people suffer from what appears to be inoperable misery. They terrorize sweet and happy people to feel better, but the feeling never lasts. They just grow more miserable over time. They are my super villains.

It is also nearly impossible to change an adult with a crappy attitude and outlook. Experiences are like the weather: unpredictable, changeable, and unavoidable. The weather almost always carries its share of merits and downsides. But there will be someone who thinks it is the most beautiful day ever, and another who cannot stand it. No matter how much you might love a snowy winter day, it is nearly impossible to convince a person over the age of 21 who hates snow to suddenly appreciate its merits. Appreciation is often learned, and some adults choose to stop learning.

However, when I'm around a 17-year-old who is angry, I know this state can be temporary. I know he or she can still change. There are even things I might be able to do to help. I can listen to them, talk about their options, maybe even get at the root of the issue and strategize ways to work through it. When I am around teenagers I feel all the emotions with a strong mixture of hope. It isn't a taxing experience, it's a positive one. I've said for years: "I have nearly endless patience for difficult teenagers, and almost zero patience for difficult adults." Now I know why.

While I was finishing my master's degree in counseling, I learned this disheartening truth: people in therapy don't change easily, and many don't change at all. There is roughly an 80% failure rate for those in addiction treatment, for example. The difficulty involved in making positive changes in the lives of others as a counselor was a tough pill to swallow. In my role as a teacher, I can safely say that 99% of my students leave my class knowing more about photography than they did when they started. A 99% success rate. Some even leave me more confident, and a few walk out with a passion for photography they didn't know they had. I realized I had a better chance at making a positive impact on the lives of others by doing what I had been doing for my entire career.

I may never use my degree in counseling professionally. I do, however, use it almost every day. Studying counseling allowed me to better understand human behavior: motivations, struggles, and pain. I also learned about behaviors that can be changed or re-directed, as well as issues and personality problems that are most likely permanent. There are people out there I can help, people I can support, and potentially people we need to be protected from. Not all bullies can change. We can only control how we respond to them, or simply stay as far away from them as we can.

I've been teaching my kids this concept for years. When my children are upset about the behavior of another child, I always tell them the same thing: "We cannot control how others act, we can only control how we re-act. And how we react teaches others about how to treat us. They either tire of us and move on or change the way they treat us." It took me decades to learn this concept, but hopefully it is reaching my kids a lot faster.

I suppose, as it relates to teaching, I'd been a super hero longer than I realized. I also must stress that when my students graduate and become adults, I don't automatically stop caring. For a mother, a child is always their child. For me, as a teacher, once a person is my student, they are always my student, which for me is a version of my own child. I can't view them as hopeless adults, just slowly growing kids.

I've also learned quite a bit from them. I get to see the growing and maturing process over and over, every year. I see how personality and sense of self develops during adolescence. I am reminded of the importance of self-discovery and the path from a middle school desire to fit in to the end of high school when many students have a firmer grasp on their individual identity. My students tend to be generally very accepting of the differences between people from a variety of countries, socio-economic backgrounds, and personal interests. The environment helps them to become comfortable with themselves. The take away is, being yourself is always better than being someone else.

When my husband died three months after our children were born I realized very soon we would never have a "normal" family structure. Yet, through my students and the modeling of various types of families, I realized my family does not need to look like any other family. My personal life does not need to copy any other. Even my career path can be uniquely mine. Most importantly, these distinct and unique areas of my life can function well outside of tradition and the norm. This powerful realization helped simplify my thoughts and allowed me to focus on working with what I have, versus comparing my life to the lives of others.

For much of my life I existed in a state of discomfort and disarray. While I may have found comfort in certain situations and in certain parts of my life, these moments were temporary and incomplete. Because I never felt like I fit, my entire being never really fit.

I've always been a slow learner. Like most people, I also learn by making mistakes. I have slowly made mistakes. Yet I do my best to learn from them, and in most areas, the learning clicks. It took a long time, but eventually things began to click. The pieces of me that seemed separate, or even at odds, began to fit together and work.

My beautiful children have been a major influential factor in pushing me to get myself in working order. It is so much easier to be a mess when you are the only one to receive the negative fallout. Through these kids I can recognize the bigger picture and see that I cannot afford to live a life in pieces if I want my family to survive. I spent much of my life in survival mode, but when I was fighting the hardest to survive I wasn't really living. I want more than survival for my family; I want us to live and to get as much out of life as we can.

My children already have some strikes against them. These sweet kids must live, essentially, their entire lives without their birth father. Whenever a classmate or friend will mention their own fathers, my children will think about the fact that they don't have their original Dad. While they have an amazing step-father, it's not the same, at least conceptually. It also places them outside the norm. Most young children, even in divorce cases, have two living parents. Yet if anyone can teach them how to happily live outside the norm, it is me.

Eventually, I will have to explain to them the nature of their father's death. While I have never lied to them, I have indicated only that he was ill when he died. And he was. I not only feel it will be important for them to know the truth for truth's sake, there is a deeper issue. My children may have addiction in their DNA and should not feel they have the "luxury" of experimenting with alcohol and drugs. I will need to do everything in my power to keep them from traveling down the same road as Chris.

The good news is we have been cultivating a pretty good relationship. I've always talked to my kids like people and done my best to explain things. I also feel I have earned their trust. So far, when I've pushed them out of their comfort zones, things have worked out. I feel confident they trust my intentions. So hopefully, when the difficult conversation comes, they will listen to what I have to say.

It took me a long time, but I figured out what really happened to their father. Why he died. It wasn't just the drugs. Chris had been a top ranked swimmer for a very long time. His parents made it possible for him to concentrate only on swimming. If he was doing well in swimming, his mother would do his shopping, his father bought him cars, and they unknowingly created a child who could only do one thing well at a time. That child became an adult who could only do one thing well, and in a complicated world of multi-tasking people, it was a recipe for disaster.

Then I came along and did the same thing for him. I helped him become a chef. I provided a place to live, I made sure that all the bills were paid, and he only had to focus on being a successful, professional cook. When I became pregnant, I abandoned him. I had to focus first on my pregnancy, and then on my premature babies. I had nothing left for him in the last months of his life.

I expected him, as an adult, to rise to the occasion, because he was their father as much as I am their mother. My intuition failed me at that time. I was so focused on my children, on their needs, that I lost the energy, the power to see what was going on inside of him.

His emotional state must have been out of control. He not only hadn't developed the skills to rise above more than one task, he hadn't developed the skills to fully stand on his own. He had no comprehension of how to take on the responsibility of three helpless lives. He knew we needed the income from his job, but we needed more than just money from him. I think he wanted to give us more, but realized it was more than he could ever handle.

That was where his anger toward me came from. Of course, the drugs were a factor, and at first, I'm sure he was simply self-medicating out of fear and desperation. Yet the drugs quickly lost the power to medicate him, and instead made things worse. They intensified the anxiety and the anger. He was in over his head and I was not there to save him. If only I had figured this out a long time ago. Though even if I had, I doubt I would have been able to change things. Chris feeling overwhelmed and scared, and his inability to handle the complexity of our life with triplets would have existed no matter what I did or said. The reality is, my powers only go so far.

I also had to learn how fruitless it was to focus on what could have been different. I spoke to a grief counselor once about my thoughts of "what if:" *What if I had called the doctor in time? What if I had insisted on drug rehab?*

She explained rather firmly, "This line of thinking cannot change what has already occurred. It does not help you, and it will not bring Chris back."

All I can do now is make sure my children go out into the world someday with the skills they need to survive on their own. This is in my head every day of my life. Even if they have my sensitivity, I know first-hand it is possible to be both sensitive and strong. This is not an easy balance to develop. Strength and resilience take work, experience, and time. But maybe, just maybe, through some of my experiences, I can pave the way for them. Make it a little smoother than the bumpy road I had to take.

There is some evidence that it is already working. A few years ago, while watching Gabby happily dance around the house, singing at the top of her lungs, I said to Craig, "I just don't get it. Gabby is nothing like I was as a child. She is so fearless and confident. So positive and free."

Craig smiled and said, "Duh, LuAnn. She isn't who you were then, she is who you are *now*."

It was probably the most wonderful thing I've ever heard. I am raising a daughter who isn't unsure of her place in the world, who knows who she is and likes herself. She's a girl who feels confident enough to dance around the house singing; someone who can find something positive in almost every situation.

This is a lesson I didn't even realize I was teaching to her. How to make the absolute best out of even the most dismal of situations. A few years ago, when our bunny ran away and we were searching the neighborhood, she stopped and said, "I know this is a sad activity, but it's also kind of an adventure!" If she has a tough morning at school, or gets hurt on the playground, she will almost always end the story with something about yummy brownies someone brought in for snack, or how pretty it was outside when she fell. Her super power appears to be a force-field that completely repels negativity.

While my boys don't necessarily have her seemingly endless supply of optimism, they are able to see outside of themselves. They don't have the self-centered tendencies many young kids have as a natural part of adolescent development. On Sundays when I put fresh sheets on the beds in the house, Charles almost always finds me and gives me a big hug. He thanks me for this task I do all the time. He also thanks me for cooking meals in the evening. Anthony can recognize how hard Craig and I work: not only how important it is, but also how tiring. He talks about how late Craig stays up grading papers, and how much he appreciates the help he gives him on homework. Anthony sometimes says to me, "Thank you Mom for always being so nice to me." He's noticed some parents yelling at their children at stores and at the park, and he realizes this is not part of his own experience.

All three kids often take the time to ask us about our day. How work is going, and how we are feeling. I honestly care more about these lessons they are learning than the grades they earn at school.

Chapter 35

Recently, my mother had a serious cancer scare. This situation rocked me to my core. After everything I had been through I could not handle the thought of losing her. I really wondered if a fresh new hell was on the horizon. I gave myself 24 hours to grieve. I cried, I expressed anger, I talked to God and cried some more. At the end of the day I brushed off the tears and thought about a way to make something good out of the situation. I knew praying was important, but it would not be enough for me in this case. I thought about what I could do to pay tribute to my mother, and what positive contribution I could make in the time she might have left.

My mother has been a huge advocate of this book. Shamefully, I hadn't worked on it for many many months. I realized one of the positive things I could do for her would be to finish writing. I fired up the computer, dusted off the files, and worked on the final chapters. This activity almost completely kept my mind off the possibility of losing my mother, my biggest supporter, my best friend.

Approximately a week later, I received the call from her that there was no cancer. A small polyp was found and removed, and my mother would be fine. I was beyond relieved. I immediately praised God because I honestly felt, once again, he answered my prayers. Maybe it was an overreaction on the part of my mother, maybe the doctor had spoken too soon, it's possible there was never anything to worry about. Whether God orchestrated the scare, or the cure, I feel he was behind the situation and knew we needed to experience it to learn and to grow.

A few months ago, my father was diagnosed with vascular dementia. Some of his symptoms include agitation, the tendency to re-write history, denial, and confusion. So, essentially, aspects of his personality that have been present my entire life, only amplified.

At first, because of his denial about the diagnosis, I would argue with him. I would point out all of his symptoms and how they proved to us the diagnosis was correct. He had dementia, and, in my mind, he needed to know that, he needed to accept it. These exchanges only managed to anger him and frustrate me. I knew better. I knew I couldn't force him to see things in any way other than his own point of view. It is possible he does not have many years left. There are few if any medical or therapeutic measures that can be taken to slow down the progression of this disease. I didn't need him to accept it. I needed to accept it.

So, I am making the best of the time he has left. I am no longer pointing out inconsistencies in his stories. I am no longer arguing with him about things he does or says. Instead, I am talking to him about things he likes to talk about. When he wants me to bring my family to visit, or to attend an event, I make the time to do so.

At first, I was doing this for him, and for my mother. To make things easier for them. But what I discovered is that this positive approach is helping me heal. I have been able to forgive the events of the past, and focus on the funny, smart man he still is. Sometimes forgiveness isn't about telling a person, face to face, that we forgive them. Sometimes forgiveness is about allowing yourself to finally let it go.

If a cure for sensitivity were discovered tomorrow, I don't think I would consider treatment. Even now, being sensitive is hard, but in a different way than it was when I was younger. Now, when someone I love is experiencing pain, or insecurity, or sadness, I have the skills and power to help them. I'm no longer the victim of pain, but a person who can help take it away.

Special Thanks

To my mother Janet, my early reader and most valued supporter. To Josh Wagner, my editor. You knew exactly what to cut, and where to dig deeper. Without you, this book would never have become what it was meant to become. To Carolyn Ellsworth-Durant, my proofreader and ray of positivity in a sometimes-dark world. To Joel Holland, my talented cover artist and little brother from another mother. To Ligeia Jennis, my sometimes proofer, sometimes sounding board, and always valued friend. To Shane Long, my main sidekick and scream partner. Distance does little to diminish our collective power. To Polly Thomas, one of my longest and dearest buds. Together we have learned how to be sensitive and kick ass simultaneously. Dennis Foreman, my work husband, and favorite highway and urban adventure partner. To Craig Culbert, my man, my love and rock. I am still in awe of the bravery required to take me on. I appreciate the strength it takes to sigh, smile, and support each of my wild plans, crazy projects, and improbable ideas. I promise you there are more to come!

Acknowledgements

While sensitivity sometimes reveals the dark side of others, it also reveals the goodness within so many. I have countless people to thank not only for this book, but for getting me through some of the toughest times in my life.

My endless appreciation to the following individuals for helping me care for my children in one way or another. Some from the early days, others as recent as last week, and many of you for support I will certainly need in the future.

Linda Adams, my sister, Aunt Fluff, my most amazing coordinator, and the woman who can make me laugh at a dangerous level. Kevin, Mickey, Alex, & Samantha Eby, aka my big brother and his team. Kaitlyn Haughey, Teagan Ubansky, Julia Fairorth, Christy Davis, Caiti Geraghty, Kat Bayard, Diana Egnatz, Nora Mayer, Anya Miller, and all my other Linden Hall girls past, present, and future.

Uncle Donald Eby, not only for the childcare and financial support, but most importantly for the weekly "adult" dinners and conversations.

Mary Lou "Mamma Moo" Nelson, Pat & Jerry Miller, Patsy Hoffer, Ruth Ann Nolt, Ruthie Westerman, Sharon & Angie Wolgemuth, Sherry & Larry Griest, Sherry Williams, Shirley & Bob Thomas, Sue Enck, Sue Thomas, Sue Thompson, Tammy & Rebecca Mill, Thelma Cairns, Therese "T-Rex" Geraghty, Andrew Geraghty, Wendi Arnold, Whitney Brown, Bob & Sue Hoffman, Christine Harvey, Christy Ewing, Diana Long, Loni Brown, Elsie Zimmerman, Gail Hawthorne, Harriet Kometa, Jackie Hagy, Jan Brown, Janet Hess, Jeanine Billett, Judy Funk, Jen Merris-Dolk, Jessie Long, Joyce Ricedorf, Kris Hostetter, Laura & Jake Sherk, Linda Kinzer, Mike & Donna Hammond, Lois Flickinger, Loni Brown, Louise Watson, Kim Funk, Nicola Cairns-Davis, Chelsea Davis, Bob & Merle Shirk, Mike & Colleen Funk, Janet Hess, Dawn Mellinger, and Marcia Landis.

This project could never have happened without the monetary and emotional support of my Kickstarter backers. The following people were instrumental in making this dream a reality:

Justin Wolfe, my most generous benefactor. No one else can Whip and Nae Nae quite like you can.

Traci Williams, my High School friend and arts supporter. Your positive spirit is vital to the lives of the sensitive.

Donna Lamoreux-Graybill, role model to Aaron and Liza, encourager of women achieving their dreams. I appreciate your excitement and support of my project.

As well as these generous supporters:

Dondria Culbert, Tiffany and Jeremy of Tiffany's beauty boutique, Serhiy Dutchak, Kelly Smith, Kelly Culbert, Chrisa "Mama Supreme" Carlson, Dan Groff, William Wrede of Meduseld Medery, Susan Milnor, and Shellee Copley.